Smart Kids

with **Learning Difficulties**

Smart Kids
with Learning
Difficulties

OVERCOMING OBSTACLES AND REALIZING POTENTIAL

Rich Weinfeld, Linda Barnes-Robinson,
Sue Jeweler, & Betty Roffman Shevitz

PRUFROCK PRESS INC.
WACO, TEXAS

Copyright © 2006 Prufrock Press Inc.

Edited by Lacy Elwood
Graphic Production by Kim Worley
Cover Design by Marjorie Parker

ISBN-13: 978-1-59363-180-2
ISBN-10: 1-59363-180-4

Library of Congress Cataloging-in-Publication Data

Smart kids with learning difficulties : overcoming obstacles and realizing
    potential / by Rich Weinfeld ... [et al.].
    p. cm.
    ISBN 1-59363-180-4 (pbk.)
    1. Learning disabled children—Education—United States. 2. Gifted
children—Education—United States. 3. Special education—United States.
I. Weinfeld, Rich (Rich Elliot), 1953-   .
LC4705.S615 2006
371.2—dc22

                                                    2005037612

Prufrock Press Inc.
P.O. Box 8813
Waco, TX 76714-8813
Phone: (800) 998-2208
Fax: (800) 240-0333
http://www.prufrock.com

To all the bright students who struggle in school and their parents and teachers who are dedicated to helping them discover their true gifts and talents. We also dedicate this book to our families—our parents, siblings, spouses, children, and grandchildren.

CONTENTS

ACKNOWLEDGEMENTS

In the beginning there was Waveline Starnes who inspired and guided us. Then, there was the compassion and support of Virginia Tucker. There was the wisdom and clarity of thinking of Joyce VanTassel-Baska. And, finally, there was the expertise and leadership of Susan Baum. We are grateful and honored to have known and worked with these four extraordinary women who have dedicated their professional lives to providing challenging programs for all students.

We also acknowledge all of the pioneers in this field whose work has provided the basis for much of our knowledge of who these kids are and what works for them, and to the teachers who have made it happen in their classrooms every day, especially Lois Baldwin, Mary Preston, Martha Abolins, Larry March, Marisa Stemple, and Dennis Higgins.

INTRODUCTION

Diamonds are rare. Two-hundred and fifty tons of rock, sand, and gravel must be processed to yield one carat of polished diamond. The diamonds we will be discussing are also rare. Bright students with learning difficulties are often not identified because their brilliance and roughness may mask one another. We see only the rough parts such as their inability to write or read effectively. What results is an attitude of discouragement and defeat. When we do find these diamonds, we must help them to shine and reach their potential by identifying their gifts and talents.

Every day, parents and teachers are challenged to find ways to empower their bright kids who, while able to participate actively in a class discussion, may be unable to write a complete sentence. They are the students who rarely have homework completed, or if done, cannot find it. They may be light years ahead in math, but reading below grade level. In contrast, these same students are the ones who may not only be able to program the computer, but completely take it apart and put it back together again. Ask them about dinosaurs, global warming, lasers, or ancient civilizations and you might get bombarded with information, but ask them to write about the same topic and they may produce little or nothing. Ask a smart student with learning difficulties to write a research paper on bridges, and he may be unable to complete the assignment. However, sitting on a table at home may be an elaborate structure this same student has built out of Legos™ or toothpicks that reflects his understanding of advanced concepts in physics, engineering, and architecture. Outside of class, these students are the creative problem solvers and analytical thinkers who show strong task commitment when the topic is personally meaningful. In school, frustrated by their inability to demonstrate academic achievement commensurate with their ability, they often have feelings of inadequacy and are at great risk of failing.

Students who are bright and underachieving, including those who are gifted and talented/learning disabled (GT/LD) must be given access to rigorous and challenging instruction. Accommodating for a student's learning disabilities or difficulties is essential. Dynamic tools can empower smart kids with learning difficulties to access appropriate instruction using their strengths, while improving and working around their weaknesses.

The purpose of *Smart Kids With Learning Difficulties: Overcoming Obstacles and Realizing Potential* is to guide parents and educators toward identifying and planning for these bright, underachieving kids so that they will reach their true potential. This book deals with research and experience the authors have gained from working directly with students who are smart, but have problems in school. We believe that the learning and teaching methods that have been applied successfully to both the gifted and talented and the learning-disabled populations can, and should, be used with all bright kids with learning difficulties, whether they have official labels or not.

This book is divided into five chapters that answer the following questions:

- Who are these kids?
- How do we find them?
- What needs to be done and who is responsible for doing it?
- What do good programs and services look like?
- What actions ensure that our bright kids will overcome their learning difficulties?

Navigating an educational system can be a challenge. A Road Map (like the one provided on p. 8) gives a visual representation of the direction that parents and educators may follow to ensure that a student will access appropriate services.

At the end of each chapter in this book is a collection of reproducible tools for parents, teachers, and students to use. They are designed to help ensure that the needs of our bright underachieving kids are met. The TIPS (To Impact Pupil Success) that appear for each tool suggest how a parent, educator, or student can utilize these supplementary materials effectively. We suggest you enlarge these tools on a copy machine and use them as part of your day-to-day interactions with smart students who face learning challenges.

When using this book and the reproducible tools within it, we suggest you:

- read the book to gain a deeper understanding of the law, population characteristics, identification, guiding principles for success, interventions, programs and services, and the actions necessary to ensure success for bright underachieving students;
- use the Road Map for assistance when navigating educational systems;
- use the book as you would a resource book, determining what information is applicable to your individual child;
- copy and use the applicable information and specific reproducible pages to help you ensure that the needs of your student are being addressed;

- give copies of appropriate information and tools to all parties involved—yourself, your child, and your child's school;
- use and create plans of action to implement successful instructional opportunities, programs, and services for your child;
- use the information as a jumping off point for further exploration on a subtopic of special interest; and
- use the reproducible pages to assist you with preparation and participation in both instructional opportunities and meetings and conferences.

TIPS and Tools: Supplementary Materials

The pages following each chapter are designed to help ensure that the needs of our bright kids with learning difficulties are met. The TIPS (To Impact Pupil Success) that appear for each tool suggest how a parent, educator, or student can use the materials effectively. In addition, some of the material within the book's text has been reproduced in easy-to-use checklists, forms, and charts, to satisfy a variety of learning styles and provide you with a quick guide to the information you need to know.

Included in this section:

•   Road Map

Road Map

What actions will ensure that our bright kids will overcome their learning difficulties? Use the Road Map (see p. 8) to see the big picture to find out where you are; where you are going; and how to get there when using this book, working to meet your child's needs, and navigating the school system.

Parents and teachers should work as partners in the process of identifying bright kids with learning difficulties and creating programming for them. This Road Map is designed so that it may be applied to your child or student. Each question and graphic on the flowchart is addressed in detail within the specific cited chapter in this book.

TIPS

Teacher:
Use the Road Map for identifying appropriate resources within your school system and pinpointing potential steps for meeting students' needs.

Parent:
The Road Map offers a look at the big picture. Use it to help navigate your child's school system. Contact the appropriate school and system personnel whenever you need help with identification procedures, interventions, programs and services, and appropriate placement for your child. Use it in conjunction with this book to find out where you are in the process and where you need to go to help your child succeed.

Student:
Use the Road Map with your parents and teachers to get the help you need when you need it.

The Road Map progresses from when you initially observe that a child has learning difficulties, to identification procedures, to programming and services decisions that need to be made, to placement in the best school setting possible and other actions that ensure success.

The ultimate destination is a place that offers kids strength-based instruction, appropriate adaptations and accommodations, and an environment that empowers students to be successful.

An asterisk (*) on the Road Map signifies the appropriate place for the implementation of any/all of the following tools and strategies (refer to Chapter 3 for more information):

- best practices
- guiding principles
- strength-based instruction
- adaptations or accommodations
- overcoming obstacles
- what works and what doesn't work
- talent development (mentor)
- roles and responsibilities

Road Map

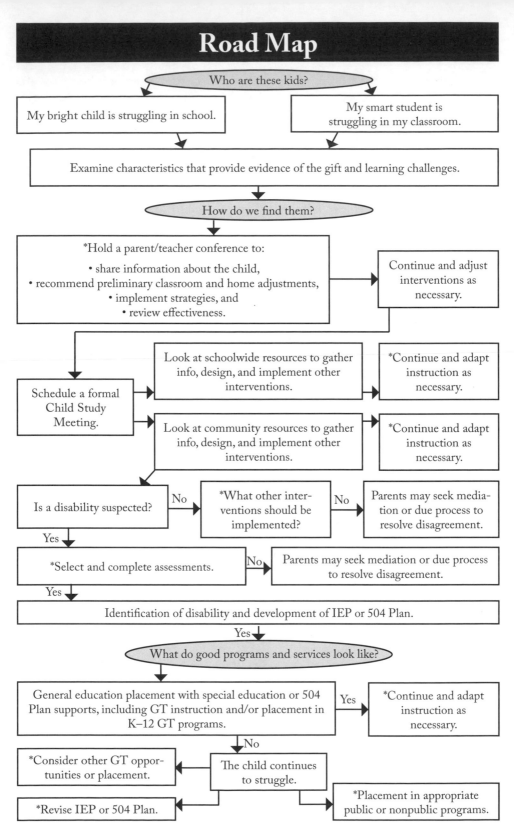

Who are these kids?

My bright child is struggling in school.

My smart student is struggling in my classroom.

Examine characteristics that provide evidence of the gift and learning challenges.

How do we find them?

*Hold a parent/teacher conference to:
• share information about the child,
• recommend preliminary classroom and home adjustments,
• implement strategies, and
• review effectiveness.

Continue and adjust interventions as necessary.

Schedule a formal Child Study Meeting.

Look at schoolwide resources to gather info, design, and implement other interventions.

*Continue and adapt instruction as necessary.

Look at community resources to gather info, design, and implement other interventions.

*Continue and adapt instruction as necessary.

Is a disability suspected?

No

*What other interventions should be implemented?

No

Parents may seek mediation or due process to resolve disagreement.

Yes

*Select and complete assessments.

No

Parents may seek mediation or due process to resolve disagreement.

Yes

Identification of disability and development of IEP or 504 Plan.

Yes

What do good programs and services look like?

General education placement with special education or 504 Plan supports, including GT instruction and/or placement in K–12 GT programs.

Yes

*Continue and adapt instruction as necessary.

No

The child continues to struggle.

*Consider other GT opportunities or placement.

*Placement in appropriate public or nonpublic programs.

*Revise IEP or 504 Plan.

1

WHO ARE THESE KIDS?

Some kids struggle. Their backgrounds, socioeconomic conditions, strengths and needs, abilities and disabilities, and their journey through life may vary, but they all struggle with learning. Some, as the following vignettes show, win the struggle and become successful individuals who make extraordinary contributions to the world.

He was from an upper-middle-class family. His mother was musically inclined and his father was an engineer. He was a very quiet child who did not speak until age 3. He hated school and disliked authority. He did poorly with rote learning. His teachers said he was a slow learner who would never amount to anything. Later, he became interested in science, math, and electrical engineering, but failed the exam for entry into an engineering program. Because of his interest in abstract and mathematical thought, he was interested in becoming a teacher. However, he believed he lacked imagination and practical ability. His name was Albert Einstein, the famous mathematician and physics genius.

She came from a socially prominent family. Her father was an alcoholic and she lived with her maternal grandparents. She had little affection for her mother who called her "Granny" because of her appearance. She was sickly, bedridden, hospitalized often, and wore a back brace due to a spinal defect. She bit her nails, had phobias, was shy, felt rejected and ugly, craved praise and attention, was insecure, and had deep feelings of inadequacy. A daydreamer, she often preferred to be isolated. After many years in school, she began to exhibit leadership qualities. She proved to be altruistic and wanted to help the elderly and poor. Her name was Eleanor Roosevelt, the famous reformer, humanitarian, and philanthropist.

He was the youngest of eight children and was of Cherokee descent. His father was a successful rancher and banker. His parents wanted him to be a minister, but he wanted to perform in a circus. He was well-coordinated, but careless in his personal hygiene. Although he excelled in history and social studies, he received poor grades in school, did not complete his work, and was expelled. His special skills included a sense of humor and recitation. His name was Will Rogers, the famous entertainer, orator, and nominee for President of the United States.

She came from a low-income family. She had two sisters; her mother was a domestic worker and her father was a minister. She was overweight, and later developed multiple sclerosis. A very quiet child, she had a certified emotional breakdown and was temporarily removed from school. However, she possessed a sense of humor, was charismatic, eloquent, humble, and a leader. Ambitious and hardworking, her name was Barbara Jordan, the famous Congresswoman and orator.

He came from a middle class family of seven children. His father was a carpenter. He had an enlarged head at birth and was not able to talk until he was almost 4 years old. He was enrolled in school 2 years late due to scarlet fever and respiratory infections. He lost his hearing and had a high-pitched voice. His attendance in school was poor. He was stubborn, aloof, shy, self-centered, and disengaged with the learning process, and he did not seem to care about school. One teacher said that his brains were addled, even though he had an excellent memory, read well, displayed perseverance, asked questions, and was a good problem solver. He liked to build things and wanted to earn money. His name was Thomas Edison, the famous inventor.

Born to an undistinguished family, he moved often with his father, sister, and brother. His mother died when he was small and his father, a farmer, remarried. He was once kicked in the head by a horse and thought dead. He had Marfan syndrome, a genetic disease that affects connective tissues, including those around the heart, skeleton, and nervous system. He briefly attended school and was considered lazy. He excelled at sports, was an avid reader, and liked practical jokes. He was a good debater and thinker and also liked to argue. Interested in sales, he wanted to open his own business. His name was Abraham Lincoln, the former President of the United States.

She was a fatherless child whose mother struggled financially. Suffering from dyslexia, she could not read, write, or do mathematical problems. Teachers described her as a class clown. She left school at age 16. Her name is Cherilyn Sarkisian LaPiere—Cher—the famous entertainer.

His teachers viewed him as bright, but inattentive and lazy. He was viewed by some of his classmates as crazy or "retarded." Each day, in elementary school, as his turn to read aloud approached, he went to the bathroom, where he got sick to his stomach and wished he would die. Unfortunately, when he returned to the room, it was always still his turn to read aloud. In sixth grade, when assigned a composition, he dictated an outstanding composition to his mother, because his poor handwriting and spelling interfered with his work production. He was accused of plagiarism, and became so disconsolate he dropped out of school for a time. In college, the student met with each of his professors prior to each semester. He described to them his love of literature and his passion for writing. He also described his need to take periodic breaks during class due to his Attention Deficit/Hyperactivity Disorder (ADHD), his need for copies of a peer's notes, his need to do all major writing on the word processor due to his written language disability, and to have books on tape because he read on a seventh grade level. The professors invariably agreed to work closely with him. Jonathan Mooney graduated from Brown University with honors and a 4.0 average. Now an inspirational speaker and author, he shares his experiences and the positive impact of appropriate adaptations and accommodations in his book, *Learning Outside the Lines* (2000).

These are profiles of famous people who were smart and overcame their learning difficulties. Think about all our kids sitting in classrooms today who are smart, but struggle in school. Their school experiences may mirror those profiled above. Unfortunately, they may not have the resilience to succeed despite their circumstances.

> *Imagine the impact if all of these kids were given the tools that could ease their struggle, and the contributions they could make if they were given the tools to succeed.*

Imagine the impact if all of these kids were given the tools that could ease their struggle, and the contributions they could make if they were given the tools to succeed.

Table 1
Definitions Related to Nonverbal Learning Disabilities

Visual-spatial: learning by seeing (e.g., diagrams, maps, graphs, facial expressions, and body language)

Organization: bringing order to self, place, and materials

Tactile-perceptual: learning through sensory input

Psychomotor: muscular activity directly related to mental processes

Population

So, who are these students and what characteristics can we look for to identify them? Bright students who are not reaching their potential present themselves in different ways, depending on what is contributing to their lack of achievement. Sometimes their difficulty in school is due to a documented learning disability. Sometimes it may be due to a health impairment such as ADHD. At other times, they may be students with neurological differences, such as Autism Spectrum Disorders, that provide challenges to their learning. In addition to the more typical learning disabilities like spelling and writing difficulties, organization, word retrieval, and processing speed, some students struggle with nonverbal learning disabilities, those characterized by problems in visual-spatial-organizational, tactile-perceptual, psychomotor, and/or nonverbal problem-solving skills (see Table 1) that adversely affect their academic performance with rigorous instruction.

Despite their outstanding abilities, smart students with learning difficulties often have problems with the physical production of schoolwork, and with the written output, organization, memory, and reading school requires. At other times, these kids seem to be average students because their brightness and their learning difficulties are masking one another. There are also students who, despite a lack of any documented disability, are underachieving, or not performing to their potential. These students are often the most difficult to understand and reach, because they do not fall into a neat category with specific instructional skills that can be addressed. Understanding who these students are, the struggles they face, how to best address their needs, and the roles parents and educators play in their lives is essential if smart kids with learning problems are to develop intellectually, socially, and emotionally.

As you become actively involved in helping your child succeed, it is important for you to have a common understanding of the definitions and terms used in both the field of gifted education and the realm of special education. The following definitions will help facilitate communication between yourself and school personnel and clarify what groups of students we are referring to in this book. This knowledge will contribute to your effectiveness and efficiency in advocating for appropriate programming and identification decisions for your child.

Definition of Gifted and Talented Students

A recent federal education policy, the No Child Left Behind Act (NCLB), defines gifted and talented students as

> students, children, or youth who give evidence of high achievement capability in areas such as intellectual, creative, artistic, or leadership capacity, or in specific academic fields, and who need services or activities not ordinarily provided by the school in order to fully develop those capabilities. (2001, p. 544)

In addition, the Jacob K. Javits Gifted and Talented Students Education Act (1988) provides us with another good definition of gifted and talented students as:

> Those children and youth with outstanding talent [who] perform or show the potential for performing at remarkably high levels of accomplishment when compared with others of their age, experience, or environ-

ment. These outstanding talents are present in children and youth from all cultural groups, across all economic strata, and in all areas of human endeavor. (Title IV, Sec. 4101)

Definition of Learning Disabilities

The Individuals with Disabilities Education Act (IDEA) was first signed into law in 1990. It was later updated in 2004. This legislation provides a good definition of learning disabilities as defined by federal law.

In general, the term *specific learning disability* indicates a disorder in one or more of the basic psychological processes involved in understanding or in using language. This includes spoken or written language. In addition, federal law notes that the disability may manifest itself in the imperfect ability to listen, think, speak, read, write, spell, or do mathematical calculations (IDEA, 1990).

Disorders considered to be learning disabilities include conditions such as perceptual disabilities, brain injuries, minimal brain dysfunction, dyslexia, and developmental aphasia (a language impairment caused by brain damage). However, federal law does not include learning problems that are primarily the result of visual, hearing, or motor disabilities, of mental retardation, of emotional disturbance, or of environmental, cultural, or economic disadvantages (IDEA, 1990).

Definition of Gifted and Talented/Learning-Disabled Students

Those students who possess an outstanding gift or talent and are capable of high performance, but who also have a learning disability that makes some aspect of academic achievement difficult are considered to be gifted and talented and learning disabled (GT/LD). Often called *twice-exceptional*, these students meet the definitions for both gifted and talented and learning-disabled students.

Definition of Gifted and Talented/ADHD Students

Some students possess an outstanding gift or talent and are capable of high performance, but also have been identified as having Attention Deficit/Hyperactivity Disorder. The criteria used by a trained professional in diagnosing ADHD is included here; however, this should not be used to diagnose your student, but should simply be considered as a guide to pinpointing students who may have problems attending.

The following definition is taken from the American Psychiatric Association's (2000) *Diagnostic and Statistical Manual of Mental Disorders-IV* (DSM-IV). The DSM-IV is the standard reference system used by mental health professionals and physicians for diagnosis of disorders. The DSM-IV defines a person with ADHD as displaying the following characteristics:

I. Person aligns with either A or B:

A. Six or more of the following symptoms of inattention have been present for at least 6 months to a point that is disruptive and inappropriate for developmental level:

i. Inattention

1. Often does not give close attention to details or makes careless mistakes in schoolwork, work, or other activities.
2. Often has trouble keeping attention on tasks or play activities.
3. Often does not seem to listen when spoken to directly.
4. Often does not follow instructions and fails to finish schoolwork, chores, or duties in the workplace (not due to oppositional behavior or failure to understand instructions).
5. Often has trouble organizing activities.
6. Often avoids, dislikes, or doesn't want to do things that take a lot of mental effort for a long period of time (such as schoolwork or homework).

7. Often loses things needed for tasks and activities (e.g., toys, school assignments, pencils, books, or tools).
8. Is often easily distracted.
9. Is often forgetful in daily activities.

B. Six or more of the following symptoms of hyperactivity or impulsivity have been present for at least 6 months to an extent that is disruptive and inappropriate for developmental level:

   i. Hyperactivity

     1. Often fidgets with hands or feet or squirms in seat.
     2. Often gets up from seat when remaining in seat is expected.
     3. Often runs about or climbs when and where it is not appropriate (adolescents or adults may feel very restless).
     4. Often has trouble playing or enjoying leisure activities quietly.
     5. Is often "on the go" or often acts as if "driven by a motor."
     6. Often talks excessively.

   ii. Impulsivity

     1. Often blurts out answers before questions have been finished.
     2. Often has trouble waiting one's turn.
     3. Often interrupts or intrudes on others (e.g., butts into conversations or games).

II. Some symptoms that cause impairment were present before age 7 years.

III. Some impairment from the symptoms is present in two or more settings (e.g., at school/work and at home).

IV. There must be clear evidence of significant impairment in social, school, or work functioning.

V. The symptoms do not happen only during the course of a pervasive developmental disorder, schizophrenia, or other psychotic disorder. The symptoms are not better accounted for by another mental disorder (e.g., mood disorder, anxiety disorder, dissociative disorder, or a personality disorder). (APA, 2000, p. 83–85)

Based on these criteria, the DSM identifies three types of ADHD: (a) ADHD, Combined Type, which is when both criteria 1A and 1B have been displayed for the past 6 months; (b) ADHD, Predominantly Inattentive Type, which occurs when criterion 1A is met, but criterion 1B has not been met for the past 6 months; and (c) ADHD, Predominantly Hyperactive-Impulsive Type, which occurs when criterion 1B is met, but criterion 1A has not been displayed for the past 6 months (APA, 2000).

Our experience has shown that some students who appear to have ADHD will no longer demonstrate the same symptoms . . . when they are given an appropriate educational environment.

Diagnosis of ADHD in gifted students can be very difficult, and should only be done by a trained professional. Some of the characteristics used to identify students who have ADHD are also characteristics of gifted students in general, gifted students who have other disabilities (including learning disabilities), and bright underachieving students. However, many gifted students, with or without other disabilities, also are impacted by ADHD. Appropriate diagnosis by a mental health professional or doctor is crucial. The identification criteria described above require that some symptoms be present before age 7, and that some impairment is present in two or more settings; this will certainly help define the existence of ADHD as a disorder separate from the child's gifts or other learning difficulties.

Our experience has shown that some students who appear to have ADHD will no longer demonstrate the same symptoms, or the same symptoms to the extent that they would be considered a disability, when they are given an appropriate educational environment. On the other hand, it has been our experience that some students will continue to demonstrate symptoms of ADHD even when the best practices of working with twice-exceptional students are in place. These students may need both medical intervention and behavioral strategies that directly address these attention issues. Parents and teachers, keep in mind that all diagnoses and any medical interventions should only be made by a trained psychiatrist, medical doctor, or other mental health professional.

Colleen Willard-Holt (1999) identified the following questions to ask when you think that your child may be showing signs of having ADHD:

- Could the behaviors be responses to inappropriate placement, insufficient challenge, or lack of intellectual peers?
- Is the child able to concentrate when he is interested in the activity?
- Have any curricular modifications been made in an attempt to change his inappropriate behaviors?
- Has the child been interviewed? What are his or her feelings about the behaviors?
- Does the child feel out of control? Do the parents perceive the child as being out of control?
- Do the behaviors occur at certain times of the day, during certain activities, with certain teachers, or in certain environments? (¶ 12)

Answering these questions will help you begin the process of determining if a disability such as ADHD may exist in the smart kid you are concerned about.

Definition of Gifted Student With Asperger's Syndrome or Autism

Gifted students with autism or Asperger's Syndrome are students who possess an outstanding gift or talent and are capable of high performance and also have an autistic disorder. Again, the American Psychiatric Association (2000) presents a definition and criteria for autistic disorders in its *Diagnostic and Statistical Manual of Mental Disorders-IV*. As with the information regarding Attention Deficit/Hyperactivity Disorder, this information is presented here only as a guide to help you determine whether you may need to seek the advice or recommendations of a trained mental health professional or doctor for your child.

The following is the criteria established by the DSM-IV for persons with autism:

A. Person displays a total of six (or more) items from criteria 1, 2, and 3, with at least two from criterion 1, and one each from criteria 2 and 3:

   1. Person displays a qualitative impairment in social interaction, as manifested by at least two of the following:

      (a) marked impairment in the use of multiple nonverbal behaviors, such as eye-to-eye gaze, facial expression, body postures, and gestures to regulate social interaction;
      (b) failure to develop peer relationships appropriate to developmental level;
      (c) a lack of spontaneous seeking to share enjoyment, interests, or achievements with other people (e.g., by a lack of showing, bringing, or pointing out objects of interest); or
      (d) lack of social or emotional reciprocity.

   2. Person displays qualitative impairments in communication, as manifested by at least one of the following:

      (a) delay in, or total lack of, the development of spoken language (not accompanied by an attempt to compensate through alternative modes of communication such as gesture or mime);
      (b) in individuals with adequate speech, marked impairment in the ability to initiate or sustain a conversation with others;
      (c) stereotyped and repetitive use of language or idiosyncratic language; or
      (d) lack of varied, spontaneous make-believe play or social imitative play appropriate to developmental level.

   3. Person displays restricted, repetitive, and stereotyped patterns of behavior, interests, and activities as manifested by at least one of the following:

(a) encompassing preoccupation with one or more stereotyped and restricted patterns of interest that is abnormal either in intensity or focus;

(b) apparently inflexible adherence to specific, nonfunctional routines or rituals;

(c) stereotyped and repetitive motor mannerisms (e.g., hand or finger flapping or twisting or complex whole-body movements); or

(d) persistent preoccupation with parts of objects.

B. Person displays delays or abnormal functioning in at least one of the following areas, with onset prior to age 3 years: (1) social interaction, (2) language as used in social communication, or (3) symbolic or imaginative play.

C. The disturbance is not better accounted for by Rett's disorder or childhood disintegrative disorder. (APA, 2000, p. 77)

The following are some of the criteria noted in children with Asperger's Syndrome (as defined by APA):

I. Person displays qualitative impairment in social interaction, as manifested by at least two of the following:

A. marked impairments in the use of multiple nonverbal behaviors such as eye-to-eye gaze, facial expression, body posture, and gestures to regulate social interaction;

B. failure to develop peer relationships appropriate to developmental level;

C. a lack of spontaneous seeking to share enjoyment, interest or achievements with other people (e.g., by a lack of showing, bringing, or pointing out objects of interest to other people); or

D. lack of social or emotional reciprocity.

II. Person displays restricted repetitive and stereotyped patterns of behavior, interests and activities, as manifested by at least one of the following:

A. encompassing preoccupation with one or more stereotyped and restricted patterns of interest that is abnormal either in intensity or focus;

B. apparently inflexible adherence to specific, nonfunctional routines or rituals;

C. stereotyped and repetitive motor mannerisms (e.g., hand or finger flapping or twisting, or complex whole-body movements); or

D. persistent preoccupation with parts of objects.

III. The disturbance causes clinically significant impairments in social, occupational, or other important areas of functioning.

IV. There is no clinically significant general delay in language (e.g., single words used by age 2, communicative phrases used by age 3)

V. There is no clinically significant delay in cognitive development or in the development of age-appropriate self-help skills, adaptive behavior (other than in social interaction) and curiosity about the environment in childhood.

VI. Criteria are not met for another specific pervasive developmental disorder or schizophrenia. (APA, 2000, p. 77)

While all students who are diagnosed with Asperger's Syndrome are high-functioning autistic students, not all high-functioning autistic students have Asperger's Syndrome. As opposed to other high-functioning autistic students, Asperger's students, by definition of the APA, do not experience a clinically significant general delay in language. However, an individual with Asperger's Syndrome may experience difficulty in understanding nonverbal, inferential, or social language, such as irony and humor.

It is important for you and your child to understand his or her own strengths and weaknesses. Gifted students with autistic disorders, including those with Asperger's Syndrome, generally have difficulties in the following areas:

- communication,
- social skills,
- range of interests,
- sensory integration, and
- behavior.

In addition, the following deficits are commonly observed in gifted students with autistic disorders, including those with Asperger's Syndrome:

- trouble focusing on what's important,
- generalization of knowledge,
- difficulty transitioning to different activities,
- difficulty with time concepts, and
- atypical/uneven development.

On the other hand, students with autistic disorders, including Asperger's Syndrome, may demonstrate great strengths, including:

- advanced reading of words (but not necessarily the same level of comprehension),
- ability to hyperfocus on an activity, and
- ability to memorize lists and facts.

Definition of Bright Underachieving Students

Many kids are smart and underachieving and could benefit from the same interventions that should be given to GT/LD kids, but they may not be identified as either gifted and talented or learning disabled. All of the strategies discussed later in this book can be used to help bright, underachieving students succeed in school.

Researchers have described the following three general themes when classifying gifted, underachieving students (Reis & McCoach, 2000):

- a discrepancy between potential (or ability) and performance (or achievement),
- a discrepancy between predicted achievement and actual achievement, and
- a failure to develop or utilize latent potential without reference to external criteria and without defining or measuring potential.

Like GT/LD students, bright, underachieving students typically demonstrate outstanding abilities in either the verbal or visual-spatial area. Despite these outstanding abilities, they typically have problems producing or completing schoolwork, particularly in the area of written output. Organization, memory, and reading also may be significantly impacted. There may be a discrepancy between what the student is able to conceptualize and what he actually produces.

The term *underachieving* has a negative connotation that does not fit some of these students. A student with a documented learning disability who is also gifted and talented may take exception to being labeled as underachieving, especially in cases when it is her disability that is impacting her level of productivity, not a lack of motivation.

Characteristics

Students with gifts who also have learning challenges that affect their performance are often misunderstood and sometimes regarded as lazy or apathetic. Although the characteristics of these students vary greatly from student to student, there are some general commonalities.

These kids are in every classroom. They may look like other kids in the class, appearing to be average learners, as their strengths and weaknesses cancel out one another, or these kids may stand out because of their poor behavior, lack of achievement, or disorganization. Smart kids with learning difficulties can be highly verbal, expressing great insights and knowledge, yet they may never complete their written work. Or, these students may contribute very little verbal expression to the class, yet they excel in hands-on activities. They may be reading below grade level and unable to remember simple directions. They may be holding it together in school, but falling apart at home. Smart students with learning challenges are likely to be experiencing problems related to some or all of the stumbling blocks that are described in detail later in this book.

Table 2 may present characteristics that look very familiar to you; it provides a list of many of the characteristics found in smart kids who struggle in school due to learning problems. You can use it to help you understand your child or student better.

Table 2
Comparison of Characteristics of Gifted Students With or Without Disabilities

Characteristics of Gifted Students Without Disabilities	Characteristics of Gifted Students With Disabilities
Ability to learn basic skills quickly and easily and retain information with less repetition	Often struggle to learn basic skills due to cognitive processing difficulties; need to learn compensatory strategies in order to acquire basic skills and information
High verbal ability	High verbal ability, but extreme difficulty in written language area; may use language in inappropriate ways and at inappropriate times
Early reading ability	Frequently have reading problems due to cognitive processing deficits
Keen powers of observation	Strong observation skills, but often have deficits in memory skills
Strong critical thinking, problem-solving, and decision-making skills	Excel in solving real-world problems; outstanding critical thinking and decision-making skills; often independently develop compensatory skills
Long attention span—persistent, intense concentration	Frequently have attention deficit problems, but may concentrate for long periods in areas of interest
Questioning attitude	Strong questioning attitudes; may appear disrespectful when questioning information, facts, etc. presented by teacher
Creative in the generation of thoughts, ideas, actions; innovative	Unusual imagination; frequently generate original and, at times, rather bizarre ideas; extremely divergent in thought; may appear to daydream when generating ideas
Take risks	Often unwilling to take risks with regard to academics; take risks in nonschool areas without consideration of consequences
Unusual, often highly developed sense of humor	Humor may be used to divert attention from school failure; may use humor to make fun of peers or to avoid trouble

Table 2, continued	
May mature faster at different rates than age peers	Sometimes appears immature because they may use anger, crying, withdrawal, etc. to express feelings and to deal with difficulties
Sense of independence	Require frequent teacher support and feedback in deficit areas; highly independent in other areas; often appear to be extremely stubborn and inflexible
Sensitive	Sensitive regarding disability area(s); highly critical of self and others including teachers; can express concern about the feelings of others even while engaging in antisocial behavior
May not be accepted by other children and may feel isolated	May not be accepted by other children and may feel isolated; may be perceived as loners, because they do not fit typical model for either a gifted or a learning disabled student; sometimes have difficulty being accepted by peers due to poor social skills
Exhibit leadership ability	Exhibit leadership ability; often leader among the more nontraditional students; demonstrate strong streetwise behavior; the disability may interfere with ability to exercise leadership skills
Wide range of interests	Wide range of interests, but are handicapped in pursuing them due to process/learning problems
Very focused interests (i.e., a passion about certain topics to the exclusion of others)	Very focused interests (i.e., a passion about a certain topic to the exclusion of others) often not related to school subjects

Note. From *Comparison of Characteristics of Gifted Students With or Without Disabilities*, by D. Higgins, L. Baldwin, & D. Pereles, 2000, Unpublished manuscript. Reprinted with permission of the authors.

TIPS and Tools:
Supplementary Materials

Included in this section:

- They Did It! So Can I!
- Characteristics of Gifted Students With Disabilities Checklist

They Did It! So Can I!

Some well-known individuals can provide inspiration for smart kids with learning disabilities, their parents, and their teachers. It helps to understand that others who we look to as successful role models have also experienced learning difficulties.

TIPS

Teacher:
Use with whole class, small group, or individual students in conjunction with a research unit integrated into the curriculum. For example, if a character in a literary piece has learning challenges, this activity will give students insight to challenges others have faced. You can help your students recognize that kids with learning challenges have great potential for success.

Parent:
Use with your child to heighten awareness that people do overcome challenges. Read about the lives of famous people with learning difficulties as a family and discuss their struggles, strategies, and successes.

Student:
Learn about others who have been able to overcome their personal obstacles. Think about how their stories relate to you. Remember, it is OK to be different.

They Did It!

The famous people on this list have all faced learning difficulties in their lives and have overcome those difficulties to be successful adults. Using this list and the directions that follow, research a famous person who has overcome his or her learning problems to become successful.

Hans Christian Andersen
Stephen Bacque
Ann Bancroft (explorer)
Harry Belafonte
Alexander Graham Bell
Stephen J. Cannell
Winston Churchill
Bill Cosby
Tom Cruise
Leonardo Da Vinci
Walt Disney
Malcolm Forbes
Henry Ford
Danny Glover
Whoopi Goldberg
Salma Hayek
Bruce Jenner

Magic Johnson
John Lennon
Jay Leno
Carl Lewis
Greg Louganis
Edward James Olmos
Pete Rose
Nolan Ryan
Charles Schwab
Steven Spielberg
Jackie Stewart
Quentin Tarantino
Lindsay Wagner
Henry Winkler
Robin Williams
Woodrow Wilson

Directions:

1. Choose a person from the list above or from another source.
2. Research information about the person.
3. Once you have collected information, create a product that informs an audience about the individual you have studied. You may:

   a. write a report,
   b. make a storyboard,
   c. design an exhibit,
   d. make a scrapbook,
   e. record information,
   f. create a video,
   g. perform a skit,
   h. create a collage, or
   i. design your own product.

Characteristics of Gifted Students with Disabilities Checklist

The following page provides a checklist of characteristics of students who are gifted, but also face learning challenges. It can be used to help identify these students.

TIPS

Teacher:
Study the characteristics checklist. Observe your students. Create a list of students in your class who exhibit these characteristics. Use the information to help identify these students; provide interventions, programs, and services; and conference with parents.

Parent:
Study the characteristics checklist. Observe your child. Share your observations and questions with your child's teacher and other staff members. Talk with your child about these characteristics and his or her strengths and weaknesses.

Student:
Talk to your parents and teachers about your strengths, interests, and needs, and how they relate to the characteristics that describe you.

Characteristics of Gifted Students
With Disabilities Checklist

❏ Often struggle to learn basic skills due to cognitive processing difficulties; need to learn compensatory strategies in order to acquire basic skills and information

❏ High verbal ability, but extreme difficulty in written language area; may use language in inappropriate ways and at inappropriate times

❏ Frequently have reading problems due to cognitive processing deficits

❏ Strong observation skills, but often have deficits in memory skills

❏ Excel in solving real-world problems; outstanding critical thinking and decision-making skills; often independently develop compensatory skills

❏ Frequently have attention deficit problems, but may concentrate for long periods in areas of interest

❏ Strong questioning attitudes; may appear disrespectful when questioning information, facts, etc. presented by teacher

❏ Unusual imagination; frequently generate original and at times rather bizarre ideas; extremely divergent in thought; may appear to daydream when generating ideas

❏ Often unwilling to take risks with regard to academics; take risks in nonschool areas without consideration of consequences

❏ Humor may be used to divert attention from school failure; may use humor to make fun of peers or to avoid trouble

❏ Sometimes appear immature because they may use anger, crying, or withdrawal to express feelings and to deal with difficulties

❏ Require frequent teacher support and feedback in deficit areas; highly independent in other areas; often appear to be extremely stubborn and inflexible

❏ Sensitive regarding disability area(s); highly critical of self and others, including teachers; can express concern about the feelings of others even while engaging in antisocial behavior

Characteristics of Gifted Students
With Disabilities Checklist, continued

❐ May not be accepted by other children and may feel isolated; may be perceived as loners, because they do not fit the typical model for either a gifted or a learning-disabled student; sometimes have difficulty being accepted by peers due to poor social skills

❐ Exhibit leadership ability; often leader among the more nontraditional students; demonstrate strong streetwise behavior; sometimes the disability may interfere with ability to exercise leadership skills

❐ Wide range of interests but are handicapped in pursuing them due to process/learning problems

❐ Very focused interest (i.e., a passion about a certain topic to the exclusion of others) often not related to school subjects

Note. From *Comparison of Characteristics of Gifted Students With or Without Disabilities*, by D. Higgins, L. Baldwin, & D. Pereles, 2000, Unpublished manuscript. Reprinted with permission of the authors.

2

How Do We Identify Smart Kids With Learning Difficulties?

Identification

Students who are bright and have learning challenges need to be carefully identified so that they can receive both the challenge and support they need and deserve. Successful identification consists of many pieces. The pieces may not make sense in isolation, but together they can eventually provide a clear understanding of an individual child's educational history, strengths, needs, and learning styles. The first step is to help those holding the individual pieces—the student, parents, teachers, and school—to recognize them and figure out how they fit together.

As a parent, you, of course, are your child's first teachers and you bear the ultimate responsibility for making educational choices. You are probably concerned about the average (or below average) performance of your child, who you know is bright, but you may not be aware of the resources that are available to you. You may not even be aware of your right to request an educational evaluation if you suspect that your child may have an educational disability that requires the provision of special education and related services. As a result, your pieces may be the last to fall into place. However, if in using the materials in this book you suspect that your child may have learning disabilities that need to be addressed by his school, a phone call to his teacher or counselor can initiate the identification process and open up discussion of your child's needs. Parents and teachers must work collaboratively to develop appropriate educational services for all children.

Regardless of the circumstances, smart students with learning challenges have repeatedly reported school as being a difficult and frustrating experience. Some student's behaviors (whether acting out or shutting down) do provide clues to their parents that the formal identification process for gifted and talented or learning disabilities should be considered. At other times, it is their teachers who are sensitive to and address these students' apparent school performance difficulties carefully and proactively through school meetings that get the ball rolling with the identification process. The importance of early identification and intervention has been well-documented. The earlier we find the kids who need additional services and the earlier we provide appropriate programming for these kids, the more successful the interventions will be.

> *The earlier we find the kids who need additional services and the earlier we provide appropriate programming for these kids, the more successful the interventions will be.*

If you are a teacher, you should have the experience and training to identify students who are having learning problems. Guiding a student and his or her family through the identification process takes time, and you must work closely with the student's parents. Collaboration is critical to begin any special testing or other intervention. The identification process is crucial to an effective delivery of services for your smart students with learning problems.

Parents and teachers, remember that students themselves are critically important members of the team. These children are a puzzle even to themselves, and are often greatly relieved when their learning difficulties are diagnosed and accommodated for, because they no longer carry the burden of fault for their lack of success in school.

Parents, teachers, and students each need to understand their position of importance in the identification process. Delivery of appropriate educational services for bright students with learning difficulties is dependent on the quality of the working relationship between these students, their parents, and their teachers.

Gifted Identification

Many school districts conduct a broad-based gifted screening process for their students during the elementary years, usually between grades 2 and 5. To ensure that all students receive a fair opportunity to be identified, it is important that all students be screened, and that no one is excluded from this process because of a disability.

There are some important principles that should be in place to ensure the screening procedures are accurate and thorough. First, schools should choose a committee that represents classroom teachers, special educators, art or music teachers, and others, including guidance counselors and media specialists. These varied perspectives and lenses are essential to compiling a complete picture of each student.

Second, keep in mind that effective screening and selection procedures use multiple criteria. Parents, teachers, and other school staff should be part of the process, and tests should include those that measure critical thinking, problem solving, and verbal and nonverbal reasoning. Recommendations from different sources and student work samples are good sources of information. Some of the best information may come from nontraditional sources, like portfolios and community nominations. It is important not to rely on only the test data and not to exclude a student because of one low indicator. We should not adhere to rigid cutoffs when evaluating performance on test data, but rather look at ranges of scores in relationship to all the other data. A complete list of tools that can be used in identifying gifted (or GT) students is included in the supplementary materials at the end of this chapter.

We must ensure that children from different backgrounds and experiences, including those with special needs and learning difficulties have a fair chance to be considered for gifted programs. Historically, gifted programs have not adequately identified and served African American and Hispanic students. In addition, girls have typically been underrepresented in rigorous math and science instruction. Today, we see an increasing trend of boys not being identified and not participating in rigorous instruction. Boys, especially minorities, continue to be disproportionably identified for special education. Advocacy on the part of staff, parents, or students must be a vital part of the process. Personal knowledge of students' strengths and interests may be more indicative of their abilities and potential than any objective assessment.

Schools that implement these principles will uphold the integrity of the screening process. However, school personnel must be ever mindful that they must continually assess children, for they grow and mature at different rates through their school years.

Parents, the school should communicate the specifics of the selection and decision-making processes to you in order to promote understanding and to build strong partnerships that will benefit your children. This communication should begin during your child's first years of schooling, for early recognition programs will foster and nurture the natural curiosity and creativity of children and serve as building blocks for future learning.

Gifted and Talented/Learning-Disabled Identification

The process used to identify students as gifted with learning disabilities varies from one state to the next, as well as in school districts within a particular state. It is important to contact your state department of education, as well as your local school district, for the current guidelines for gifted identification. However, the process for identifying disabilities is governed by federal law. This law has recently changed with implications that we will discuss later. The following is a discussion of some of the guidelines and practices used in a few states. Parents and teachers, we offer this discussion as a way to familiarize yourself with some of the guidelines already established by some school districts. However, you should contact your local school district and state department of education to get a full listing of their own guidelines and practices for identifying gifted students with learning disabilities.

Maryland is one of a few states to offer special guidelines for identifying GT/LD students. GT/LD students are often identified as learning disabled through special education procedures (Maryland State Department of Education [MSDE], 2000). Currently, when students are evaluated for a suspected learning disability, information becomes available about their strengths and challenges. The information revealed in IQ testing may serve to identify students as gifted who otherwise might have gone unidentified. People are often surprised to discover a broad verbal or performance IQ score that is in the superior or very superior range, indicating evidence of superior abilities, especially when they have previously seen the daily struggle that a student is experiencing. At other times, a careful look at the subtests in the IQ testing shows significant gifts while, as a result of students' weaknesses averaging out their strengths, the broad verbal or performance scores look unremarkable.

Using the IQ and educational discrepancy range (a significant gap between achievement and aptitude) is one consideration among many when determining if a child qualifies as having a learning disability. Maryland's learning disability identification guidelines include students who are functioning in the superior and very superior range (Maryland State Department of Education, 2001).

For example, a student who scores in a very superior range (130) on an intelligence test, but scores only average (100) on an education achievement test, would be said to have a significant discrepancy or difference. This difference is one indication that the student may have a learning disability.

Maryland is just one state to establish guidelines for identifying gifted/learning-disabled students. Other states and organizations have also set up parameters for identifying these students. For example, in a letter to the Learning Disabilities Association of North Carolina, a representative of the United States Department of Education offered guidelines for the identification of GT/LD students, including:

- No child's IQ can be too high for that child to be considered for eligibility for special education services.
- Children can be considered for special education if they are not working at their ability level. To determine this, they must be given the opportunity to work at their ability level.
- We must take into consideration what the child's performance would be without the help and support of parents and outside providers like tutors and therapists (T. Hehir, personal communication to P. Lillie and R. Felton, April 5, 1995).

These guidelines have been reaffirmed in a Pennsylvania District Court (*West Chester Area School District v. Chad C.*, 2002), which stated that:

- students' grades that are declining (even if not failing) are not a reflection of their ability, and
- one must consider the child's potential when determining if he or she qualifies for service.

Notice that both the U.S. Department of Education's guidelines directed toward North Carolina's Learning Disabilities Association and those followed by the Maryland State Department of Education described on the previous page incorporate the use of IQ tests.

Although IQ tests are commonly used to help determine a child's giftedness, they are not and should not be the only method used to identify a student's strengths. Many school systems have developed and adopted additional ways to determine a child's giftedness.

Some GT/LD students have been and will continue to be identified by gifted screening processes. Keep in mind that for others, the masking of their giftedness by their learning difficulties will leave them unidentified by general screening processes. It is crucial that the professionals who are identifying giftedness be familiar with characteristics of GT/LD students, as well as with the screening data for patterns that may suggest a gifted student with disabilities. Only an authorized school team can make the final determination that a child has a learning disability.

In addition to screening committees, IEP (Individualized Educational Plan) teams must take special caution during the process of identifying gifted students with learning disabilities (Maryland State Department of Education, 2001). Consideration should be given to the unique profiles of GT/LD kids who present some strengths and, at first look, may not appear to need services.

Teams must recognize that a student may be gifted or have far above average ability and also have a specific learning disability. The specific learning disability may be manifested in an inability to complete class work at the level expected, given the student's high cognitive ability, without tutoring or support. Like students with learning disabilities, these gifted students may have organizational or processing weaknesses that make it difficult to achieve classroom expectations. For example, a student may have completed the homework, but cannot find it to hand in to the teacher or the student may turn in an outline rather than paragraphs because the student missed part of the directions.

In order to be identified with a specific learning disability, high-ability students should display evidence of a discrepancy between their cognitive ability and their achievement. For example, a student who is able to talk in detail about something, but can't write the same ideas on paper shows such a discrepancy. Although a discrepancy between ability and achievement should not be the only measure of a learning disability for high ability students, it should be carefully considered as one indication that a disability exists (Brody & Mills, 1997).

These identification procedures can provide us with a guide to find GT/LD students. However, there are still inherent stumbling blocks to overcome in order to officially identify smart kids with learning disabilities as GT/LD in the schools.

Potential Stumbling Blocks to GT/LD Identification

First, there are students who are originally identified for their giftedness, while any learning disability they may have goes unnoticed, because of their ability to compensate for their weaknesses. The disability or question of disability usually arises as the demand for written work increases in school. For example, in the primary grades (K–3) a student may appear bright because of his or her advanced vocabulary and oral expression, but when the writing demands increase, the student continues to use simple words and sentences.

Then, there are those students who are identified first by their learning disabilities; as a result, all of the attention given to them in school is directed at remediation. For example, students who are not able to read may be identified as needing special education services, leaving their teachers to never see evidence of their gifts. Inadequate assessments or depressed IQ scores often lead to an underestimation of their intellectual abilities. The result is that their areas of giftedness are not recognized or addressed. The severity of the learning disability is masking their giftedness. Only if and when a teacher or parent sees the spark of high ability in other areas is there a chance that these students' gifts are revealed.

And, there are those students who may appear to be of average ability, because they are using all of their gifts to compensate for their areas of weakness. The giftedness and the learning disability are masking each other. These students are not getting services for either their gift or their disability.

> *Only if and when a teacher or parent sees the spark of high ability in other areas is there a chance that these students' gifts are revealed.*

Finally, there are those students who may have been identified as gifted, yet are exhibiting difficulties in school and are considered to be underachievers. They may be working at or near grade level. Their underachievement is often attributed to poor self-concept, lack of motivation, or laziness. Their superior gifts are masking their learning disability.

Regardless of the scenario, these students often carry with them a low self-concept because of the inner conflict they face—they know they are bright, but at the same time they are feeling frustrated by their shortcomings. Less easy to define, but equally important to identify, are students who are bright and experiencing learning challenges, but who do not qualify for the GT, GT/LD, LD, or other label—the bright underachieving students.

Identification as GT/ADHD
or GT/With Autism Spectrum Disorders

The identification of a student as both gifted and having either ADHD or autism spectrum disorders requires cooperation between parents, psychologists and/or doctors, and educators. Information from intelligence tests, home performance, and school performance checklists will provide evidence of the student's gifts. Behavioral checklists, expert analysis, and a combination of both objective and anecdotal evidence from the classroom will need to be compiled and carefully considered to determine if an educational disability is present.

Recognizing
and Freeing Potential

Now that you've been given some background on the identification process, it's up to you as a parent to recognize the potential your child possesses. You probably already know your child is bright, but how do you work to unleash her potential and help her succeed despite her learning difficulties? The next section will help you pinpoint your child's potential for success in a few specific areas, ultimately aiding him in overcoming his obstacles and realizing his potential. In addition, the ORR charts (see below) presented in this section and in the supplementary materials at the end of this chapter can be given to your child's school when completed for consideration during the gifted or gifted/learning disabled screening processes.

The dictionary defines *potential* as "power; existing in possibility; capable of development into actuality." Potential may be an internal passion, it may be determined by circumstances and opportunities, or it may be a combination of all of these ideas.

Children give us clues that help us recognize their potential. As parents and teachers, we need to open our eyes to the everyday actions of our children. One process that can help kids find their power is called Observe and Reflect and Respond (ORR). ORR is a model for parents and educators to think about and act on children's behaviors. Observing and reflecting on behaviors in each of the following categories of characteristics can alert adults to the presence of potential. Once the behaviors are recognized, appropriate responses may help that potential become performance (Barnes-Robinson, Jeweler, & Ricci, 2004).

When observing and reflecting about children, it is helpful to begin by understanding what each of the following categories of characteristics mean in order to organize our thinking. The ORR charts detail a child's actions in each of the following categories:

- *Thinking (cognitive)* is the process of logical thought. It is the act or process of knowing. Children often let us know what they are thinking about. They may tell us in words and/or show us through their actions and behaviors.
- *Responsibility (commitment)* occurs when a person is able to answer for their conduct or follow through on an agreement to do something. Children often show us through their actions and behaviors that they can start and finish a task or that they deeply care about something.
- *Breaking work into parts (task analysis)* is the ability to understand the steps to follow in order to complete an assigned piece of work. Your children may demonstrate that they understand how to successfully complete tasks.
- *Creative ability (imagination)* is when a person has a command of imagery and is able to be inventive. Children share their creations of the mind in a variety of ways, through the visual arts, music, literature, poetry, and architecture or engineering.
- *Appreciation of beauty (aesthetics)* is when an individual responds to beauty and the arts. Children can let us know

verbally, nonverbally, and artistically that they recognize beautiful things.

- *Interactions with others (social)* can be defined as the cooperative and interdependent relationships of an individual with the members of a group. Children can be observed as they engage in activities with others and give insights into the interpersonal and intrapersonal selves (Barnes-Robinson et al., 2004).

The ORR charts that follow as Table 3 offer specific examples under each of the six categories. The first column describes a specific observable behavior you make about the child, the second column lists questions that you can ask yourself during reflection time, and the third column offers possible responses that may free the potential observed in the child. These are some examples designed as jumping off places for individualized responses.

What frees potential? Social, emotional, and sensory experiences shape the brain in the early years more than information. Our culture shapes us in the early years, too. That is when the brain has the most capacity to organize itself, taking advantage of all its neurons to lay the framework for language, music, math, and art. The cells do not engage in learning if there aren't opportunities, and without opportunities the possible connections are never made (Barnes-Robinson et al., 2004).

A child's potential can be freed in different ways, including perceiving opportunities, recognizing requisite skills, and working in a positive climate. Potential is realized when there is motivation to work hard, and when there is an attainable goal in sight. It can be unlocked when there is someone who believes in you, someone who guides, supports, and expects you to succeed. Potential is realized where there is sheer will, and when there is faith in a future. It is unleashed when there is someone to nurture and develop a skill or talent in a child, even when there is little economic opportunity. And, potential is recognized when a child sees someone she loves overcome the impossible to achieve something important.

Our role, as parents and teachers, is to offer guidance and direction to our children so they will explore their talents and realize their gifts. The ORR process can provide specific ideas that give inspiration, stimulation, and affirmation to children (Barnes-Robinson et al., 2004).

Table 3
Completed ORR Charts

Thinking (Cognitive)

Observe	Reflect	Respond
Sits alone and looks through reading materials for hours.	Does my child enjoy learning about things? What is my child interested in? Does my child understand what is read?	Ask questions about my child's reading materials. Collect books and articles that would interest my child. Provide a variety of reading materials to my child.
Asks questions about anything and everything.	What is my child curious about? How can I help my child answer questions?	Gather materials with my child to find answers to questions. Talk with my child about possible answers. Choose guiding questions to help my child answer question.
Finds connections and relationships between things.	What is the process my child uses to see connections?	Ask my child for observations of what is common or different between things. Ask my child to explain how the connections were made.
Remembers things that I forget.	Does my child have a strong memory?	Play memory games with my child. Memorize and recite poems and songs together.

Responsibility (Commitment)

Observe	Reflect	Respond
Brings home animals in need of care.	Does my child have an interest in animals? Does my child feel responsible for the animals?	Introduce my child to books about animals. Take my child to interview a veterinarian. Suggest helping a neighbor with a pet.
Tries hard even though mistakes are being made.	Does my child complete difficult tasks? Does my child deal well with frustration? Is my child persistent? Is my child a perfectionist?	Praise my child's efforts. Explain that a good way to learn is from our mistakes.

Table 3, continued

Responsibility (Commitment), continued

Observe	Reflect	Respond
Finishes a project independently.	Is my child able to work alone? Do I help my child more than I need to?	Praise my child for completing tasks. Give my child added responsibilities at home.
Talks about helping people.	What opportunities could I offer my child to meet this need?	Join service organizations. Volunteer in the community. Discuss issues about fairness.
Is always ready for school on time.	Does my child take responsibility for himself?	Give my child additional opportunities for independence. Praise my child's organizational skills.

Breaking Work Into Parts (Task Analysis)

Observe	Reflect	Respond
Explains how to play a complex game.	Is my child capable of doing more complicated tasks than I though possible?	Let my child explain the steps in a task to a younger sibling. Play complex games with my child. Ask my child to help me solve a problem.
Finishes long-term school projects with ease.	What time management skills does my child use?	Allow my child to become involved in extracurricular activities. Ask my child to help plan family activities.
Keeps a neat and organized bedroom.	Is this carried over to other aspects of my child's life?	Ask my child to help organize issues or needs around the house. Assist my child in transferring these skills to other areas when needed.
Recognizes different ways to solve the same problem.	Are my child's ideas more effective and efficient ways of solving a problem? Does my child see solutions in a different way?	Reinforce my child's unique thinking. Ask my child to explain the steps used to solve the problem.

Creative Ability (Imagination)

Observe	Reflect	Respond
Sits and plays make believe games.	Do my child's toys promote pretend play? Should I get involved during this play?	Acknowledge the value of the play. Get involved in the play. Introduce new scenarios to the play.
Draws pictures on the sidewalk, scraps of paper, and in the sand at the beach.	Does my child have an interest in drawing? How can I promote this interest?	Ask my child to draw something specific for me. Show examples of many kinds of drawing. Introduce different materials for drawing. Take my child to an art gallery.
Dances around the house to music in his or her head.	Does my child enjoy moving to a beat?	Clear a special space for my child to dance. Play a variety of music to move to. Ask if my child would like to take dance lessons.
Has fun playing with "any old stuff" around the house.	Is my child able to think about everyday objects in a different way?	Use questions to promote creative thinking about the items he plays with. Make suggestions: "Can you think of another use for this potato masher?"
Makes up stories about every day things.	How can I encourage this creativity without being judgemental? How do I nurture original thinking?	Encourage my child to be creative with stories. Ask questions that will force my child to give more details. Encourage my child to write stories down or dictate them to me.

Appreciation of Beauty (Aesthetics)

Observe	Reflect	Respond
Tells you about a beautiful sunset.	Does my child comment often about beauty in nature? Is my child observant?	Talk about colors, form, and composition in nature. Point out aesthetically pleasing things in the environment.

Appreciation of Beauty (Aesthetics), continued

Observe	Reflect	Respond
Recognizes beauty in art and architecture.	Does my child observe the environment for things of beauty?	Take my child to art galleries and museums. Take art books out of the public library for my child. Take a city architecture tour.
Is always listening to music.	What is it about the music my child appreciates? What kinds of music does my child listen to?	Take my child to a concert. Share my personal music library with my child.

Interactions With Others (Social)

Observe	Reflect	Respond
Sits by an aging relative and cuddles for a long time.	Does my child think about others' needs first?	Let my child know that the affection shown to the relative is important.
Has good friends.	What attributes does my child have that attracts good friends? Does my child prefer fewer good friends rather than many?	Create play dates for my child. Talk about the value of friendship. Read books about friendship.
Enjoys listening to and telling family stories.	Is my child family oriented? What will encourage my child's interest in family?	Arrange for family get-togethers. Write the family stories into a book.
Leads others.	What leadership qualities does my child have?	Allow my child to lead the family in an activity over the weekend. Enroll my child in leadership activities.

Note. From "Potential: Winged Possibilities to Dreams Realized!" by L. Barnes-Robinson, S. Jeweler, and M. C. Ricci, June 2004, *Parenting for High Potential*, pp. 20–25. Copyright ©2004 by National Association for Gifted Children. Reprinted with permission.

What inspires a child to want to try something new, practice a skill, and be persistent? A writer, athlete, inventor, artist, parent, or teacher may provide inspiration to our children. Other external sources of inspiration may include the drive for success, rewards, fame, and money. It is our response as parents and educators that can inspire a child to do better, try something new, learn from his mistakes, or help others.

Two other aspects of freeing potential are stimulation and affirmation. Many children need to be jumpstarted to begin a task or pursue an interest. A positive statement of encouragement from a peer, parent, or instructor can contribute to unleashing their potential. The reinforcement takes place through our words and our actions. This support acts as an affirmation for the child. Affirmation builds confidence and confidence frees children to become risk takers (Barnes-Robinson, Jeweler, & Ricci, 2004).

The Law

Once your child's potential strengths have been noted, these can be considered in the gifted or GT/LD identification process. If your child has been identified as either gifted, GT/LD, or learning disabled, it's important for you to know your child's rights and his school's responsibilities under the law. This section will give you an overview of those legal rights and responsibilities, and hopefully provide you with the information you need to know to advocate for your child and the services she needs and deserves.

The concepts of gifted and talented and learning disabled are defined in federal and state laws. Although there is no specific legal mandate to serve those students who are GT/LD, a close look at the laws related to both giftedness and learning disabilities reveals language that can provide parents and staff with the support and guidance they need in order to effectively advocate for services. Several laws and policies refer to gifted students and students who are gifted with learning disabilities. A brief discussion of how the laws and policies may be interpreted to support the appropriate education of bright students with learning difficulties is also included below.

Gifted Students

Federal education policy defines gifted and talented students in terms of students who show evidence of their high achievement capability. Students who are gifted and simultaneously learning disabled certainly show evidence of a high achievement capability if those gathering the evidence know what to look for. It is crucial that those who are making the decisions about these capabilities understand how the disability may mask the gift and what these capabilities may, in fact, look like in students who are both gifted and learning disabled.

The federal and state governments monitor the annual yearly progress of students, according to a number of different measures. States would certainly benefit by identifying more GT/LD students as gifted and providing them with access to Advanced Placement and college preparatory programs. It will be crucial for states to help local school districts know how to identify these students and to understand how to help these students succeed once they are placed in rigorous programs.

Many states had previously adopted some of the key concepts of the definition of gifted and talented students found in the Jacob K. Javits Gifted and Talented Students Education Act of 1988. The word *potential* in the Javits definition is very significant for GT/LD students, many of whose assessments and achievements provide evidence of their potential.

The services that are offered for gifted and talented students vary widely from state to state, with some states going as far as requiring an IEP (Individual Educational Plan) for all gifted students, while other states have no mandate for gifted instruction. Several states have the same legal requirement (Child Find) for finding all gifted students who reside within their jurisdiction, whether they are in public or private schools. Parents and school personnel should check with their state department of education to see where their state stands in relation to gifted mandates and child find requirements.

Students With Learning Disabilities

There has been a major change in federal law regarding the method of determining whether a child has a specific learning disability. Schools are no longer required to take into consideration whether a child has a severe discrepancy between achievement and intellectual ability. Instead, schools may use a process that determines if the child responds to scientific, research-based interventions. This change may have a great impact on students who are GT/LD. It relieves school systems from the requirement to perform assessments in order to determine if a gifted student's school performance may be discrepant from the student's superior to very superior ability. On the other hand, school systems, although not required to do so, may still choose to do this type of testing and may also consider these discrepancies if they see evidence in either their own assessments or a private assessment provided by the student's parents.

It will be up to you, the parents, to show that your student does qualify for the specific learning disability designation when she is not responding to scientific, research-based interventions. More than ever, it will be crucial to document the interventions that are being used and the evidence of how your child is responding to the interventions over time. As a parent, you will want to ask for a specific timetable that describes when and how the effectiveness of the interventions will be measured, and you will need to know what the schools will be using for documentation. You may want to collect your own samples of your child's work over a period of time that will demonstrate whether or not she is acquiring the targeted skills. Curriculum-based assessments, district and statewide testing, and the traditional psychoeducational assessments can all still be a part of this documentation. Parents and educators of students who have demonstrated evidence of giftedness, but are performing at or below average in some or all of their academics should be aware that there may be a specific learning disability present.

Gifted and Learning Disabled

One promising part of the Individuals with Disabilities Education Act 2004 update is that gifted and talented students who are disabled were included in the groups of students whose needs have priority in the U.S. Department of Education grants to guide research, personnel preparation, and technical assistance. This is the first time that IDEA acknowledges the needs of twice-exceptional children. This opens the door for more attention and potentially more services to be provided for

GT/LD students. States, local school districts, and universities will now be eligible to receive federal money to study and promote promising practices for these students. You will want to encourage your local and state school districts to be part of the research and staff development that will be available to benefit bright students with learning difficulties.

Current regulations, in most states, require that part of the determination of a specific learning disability comes from looking at whether or not the child achieves at a level that would be expected by looking at both his age and ability level, when provided with learning experiences appropriate for those age and ability levels. Including the words *ability level* in these regulations has been very helpful in the process of determining that GT/LD students do qualify for services. Students who are gifted and talented should be provided learning experiences that are appropriately rigorous. Often, only when access to rigorous instruction is provided do the student's challenges become evident. If this reference to ability level is removed from state regulations, you, the parents of a GT/LD student, must continue to advocate for access to appropriately challenging instruction for your child, but keep in mind that you will have lost a powerful legal argument for doing so. You should be aware that states will be rewriting their regulations and local school districts may be rewriting their policies as a result of IDEA's 2004 update. Parents and advocates will want to work to preserve the concept that students' performance should be compared not just to their age level, but to their ability level, as well.

> *Students who are gifted and talented should be provided learning experiences that are appropriately rigorous. Often, only when access to rigorous instruction is provided do the student's challenges become evident.*

A representative of the U.S. Department of Education provided its opinion regarding the identification of gifted students as learning disabled (see p. 30 for more information) in a letter to the Learning Disabilities Association of North Carolina. In addition to saying that no student's IQ can be too high for the child to be considered eligible for special education services, the department went on to support the concept regarding ability-level learning experiences described above. The education department also stated that it is appropriate for the multidisciplinary team to consider information regarding outside or extra instructional help or support that "may indicate that the child's current educational achievement reflects the service augmentation, not what the child's achievement would be without such help" (T. Hehir, personal communication to P. Lillie and R. Felton, April 15, 1995).

Over time, new laws and decisions from the U.S Department of Education may take the place of existing opinions. As discussed above, you will need to pay careful attention to new federal and state regulations and policies to see if they preserve the importance of the words *potential* and *ability level* as part of the consideration for determining qualification for special education services. In terms of the extra support the students may be receiving, it would seem that any outside or extra help and support that you may be providing should continue to be considered when determining if your child is responding to interventions. For example, an IEP team should consider what your child's progress in reading may have been over the past year had you not provided intensive tutoring after school.

In conclusion, it is important to keep in mind that experts have estimated that as many as 2–5% of all students are likely to fit the classification of GT/LD (Dix & Schafer, 1996; Whitmore, 1981). These figures have been substantiated in Montgomery County, MD, where 2% of all students have been identified as simultaneously gifted and disabled. As the National Association for Gifted Children (NAGC; 1998) says in its position paper "Students with Concomitant Gifts and Learning Disabilities" that, "without appropriate identification and services, the gifts of these students may never be developed" (¶ 6). You must continue to work to ensure that bright students with learning challenges have a fair opportunity to be identified as gifted. Secondly, parents and advocates must continue to look at discrepancies between your child's gifts and his academic performance. Finally, you must insist that the difference between the potential evidenced by your child's gifts and the performance evidenced by her learning challenges be the first step that alerts others to the possibility of learning disabilities.

IEP vs. 504 Plan

Under federal legislation, students who are determined to have learning disabilities may qualify for an Individualized Educational Plan (IEP). Part of the eligibility determination is based on a decision regarding whether or not your child requires specially designed instruction to meet the unique needs resulting from her disability. When it is decided that she does have a disability and needs special instruction for this disability, an IEP will be developed. The IEP includes goals and objectives and provides a specific plan for direct instruction as needed. The IEP also includes classroom and testing accommodations.

Another alternative for gifted students with disabilities is the development of a 504 Plan. Like an IEP, a 504 Plan is a result of federal law, and can put into place formal accommodations to be used both in the classroom and in testing situations. Unlike an IEP, 504 Plans do not typically provide for special education instruction of any kind. They are administered and monitored by the general educators in the school, typically the guidance counselor.

While the criteria for determining eligibility for an IEP under IDEA will primarily focus on your child's response to intervention, the standard for determining eligibility for a 504 Plan will continue to be how well your child performs compared to the average student. For most gifted students, a strict interpretation of this law will disqualify them from receiving services. Even with the impact of a disability, most gifted students perform as well as the average student. For those who do not perform at this level, a 504 Plan can provide the accommodations that level the playing field to provide equal opportunity. A 504 Plan does not typically provide the direct special education instruction that comes with the identification of a disability and the development of an IEP. This direct special education is crucial for many twice-exceptional students. You should be aware, however, that schools will sometimes be more willing to develop a 504 Plan than an IEP, because the 504 Plan will typically demand less resources from the school.

TIPS and Tools: Supplementary Materials

Included in this section:

- Identification Data Gathering Tools
- Recognizing and Freeing Potential Blank Template
- Report to Parents

Identification Data Gathering Tools

It is critical that multiple measures are used to help us find our smart kids with learning differences. These measures tap into verbal and nonverbal strengths, reading and math abilities, and other strengths that kids share through their talents and interests. This information should be gathered from parents, kids, teachers, and community members who see kids from a variety of perspectives.

TIPS

Teacher:
Find out the specific tools that are available to you when identifying students. Work with appropriate staff members to collect data about this student population. Learn how the data impacts instruction. Implement the appropriate strategies with students. Interpret the data to understand the instructional implications.

Parent:
Find out the specific tools used by your school for identification purposes. When advocating for your child, ask questions regarding the tools that may be used for your child. Understand your rights within this process.

Student:
Talk to your teachers and parents if you have questions about how the school learns what you know and how you learn best.

Identification Data Gathering Tools

Here are some examples of tools that can typically be used in identifying GT students:

_____ **Subjective and Objective Information:**

- Verbal and nonverbal test data
- Teacher and parent checklists
- Nominations: parent, staff (school specialists), peer, student, community (coaches, music/dance teachers, religious teachers, etc.)
- Portfolios/work samples

_____ **Formal Data** (These tests are given by way of example rather than as definitive because individual instruments can change over time.):

- Achievement tests (California, Iowa)
- Aptitude/ability tests
- Nonverbal reasoning tests (Naglieri Test of Nonverbal Reasoning, Raven—Standard Progressive Matrices)
- Educational assessments (Woodcock Johnson, WIAT)
- Psychological assessments (WISC-IV, Stanford Binet, etc.)
- Connor's Scales (Attention)
- Teacher checklists (Renzulli Hartman Behavioral Checklist)
- Teacher and parent rating scales (SIGS)

_____ **Informal Data:**

- Nominations from parents, staff
- Portfolios/work samples
- Teacher observations
- Preassessment data

_____ **Nontraditional Data:**

- Community nomination
- Interview
- Peer nomination
- Student nomination

_____ **Potential Charts:**

- ORR Charts

Recognizing and Freeing Potential Blank Template

The everyday observations of behavior provide us with valuable information about our kids' potential. Parents and teachers can copy and fill in the following blank chart (or multiple charts, if needed) with specific examples under each of the six categories of the ORR process: thinking, responsibility, breaking work into parts, creative ability, appreciation of beauty, and interactions with others. Note: The chart is adapted from Barnes-Robinson et al., 2004.

TIPS

Teacher:
Learn and use the ORR process to gather additional information about students. Use the information to give students curricular opportunities to unleash their potential. Use the information as a hook for motivating students. Teach students to use the process in order to build self-efficacy and self-advocacy skills.

Parent:
Learn and use the ORR process to gather additional information about your child. Use the information to give your child opportunities at home to unleash his potential. The information can act as a hook for motivating your child. Teach your child to use the process in order to build self-efficacy and self-advocacy skills. Gather information about your child and take it to a parent-teacher conference.

Student:
Learn and use the ORR process to gather additional information about yourself. Use the information to give yourself opportunities at school and at home to unleash your potential. Practice an "I can!" attitude. Be a self-advocate and tell parents, teachers, coaches, etc. who you are and what you can do.

Recognizing and Freeing Potential Blank Template

ORR Category: _____

Observe	Reflect	Respond

Report to Parents

While gathering pieces of information during the identification process, use this form to summarize information in order to provide a clear understanding of an individual child's educational history, strengths, needs, and learning styles.

TIPS

Teacher:
Work with parents to complete the form. Share with responsible staff.

Parent:
Work with teachers to complete the form. Use as guidelines for next steps.

Student:
Work with parents and staff to understand the information gathered about you.

Report to Parents

Student name:

Review of student records, including the following:

Recommendations for additional needed information:

Analysis of child's strengths and needs based on record review:

Information about specific educational programs:

Additional resources and related services:

Short-term action plan:

Long-term action plan:

Persons responsible for action plans and services:

Follow-up:

3

WHAT NEEDS TO BE DONE FOR SMART KIDS WITH LEARNING DIFFICULTIES AND WHO IS RESPONSIBLE?

Guiding Principles that Promote Success

What we do for bright students with learning difficulties is only part of the equation. *How* we do "the what" is just as important. In the right climate, where students know and feel they are respected and valued for their uniqueness, anything is possible. When students perceive they are devalued, the interventions, however appropriate, may fail. The goal of education is to provide opportunities for students to build knowledge, skills, and positive attitudes in order to become successful, contributing members of a global society. Successful, practical programming is based on solid research and theory.

These students must be guaranteed access to accelerated and enriched instruction that maintains the rigor and high standards expected of all gifted students. Bright students with learning challenges are, therefore, not to be excluded from this promise. Parents, keep this in mind when you review the information included in this chapter. Although much of this chapter is geared toward guiding teachers and the school system, you can use this information to your advantage—to advocate successfully for the school environment and experiences your child deserves and needs. You may also want to share the information and tools included in this chapter with your child's teacher.

Best Practices

The best practices for educating smart kids with learning problems can be summarized in four major components:

- instruction in the student's area of strength;
- opportunities for the instruction of skills and strategies in academic areas affected by the student's challenges;
- an appropriately differentiated program, including individualized instructional adaptations and accommodations systematically provided to students; and
- comprehensive case management to coordinate all aspects of the student's individual educational plan.

Research and a review of successful programs indicate that the most important component of these students' education is providing rigorous instruction in each student's area of strength. It is important that the instruction emphasizes problem solving, reasoning, and critical thinking, as well as includes extension and elaboration of the regular curriculum. Classroom organization must be flexible, yet structured with opportunities for collaborative goal setting, significant peer interactions, and cooperative learning. Students must receive this rigorous instruction in the least restrictive environment where they can receive educational benefit. In order to benefit from this instruction in a typical classroom setting, these students need educators to utilize appropriate strategies. Implementing these strategies involves close collaboration between special educators and general educators. By receiving appropriate instruction these students can develop their full potential (Baum, Emerick, Herman, & Dixon, 1989).

Smart kids with learning disabilities need instruction of skills and strategies in academic areas that are affected by the student's weakness or disability. Instruction is generally needed in one or more of the following areas: writing, reading, math calculations, organizational skills, test-taking skills, self-determination skills, and social skills. Research indicates that only a very small percentage of students are resistant to instruction that can greatly improve their performance in the academic areas affected by their disability. These improved skills allow GT/LD students even greater success in the development of their strengths. Skills and strategy instruction are accomplished through direct instruction and/or integrated into content instruction. Instruction in this area helps students to develop an awareness of their strengths and weaknesses and an ability to advocate for what they need in order to be successful.

Teachers need to adapt their program by utilizing a multisensory approach that emphasizes a student's strengths and interests. One successful example of this approach is the integration of art and drama into the curriculum within the middle school Center Program in Montgomery County, MD, that serves as a model for general education (see Chapter 4). An award-winning partnership with a local art college has integrated art and drama into all curricular areas, resulting in students demonstrating both a greater motivation and a greater mastery of the curricular objectives. An art specialist from the college works with teachers to identify key concepts in content areas and find ways that art can be used in both learning activities and assessment. In all of the Montgomery County Public Schools (MCPS) GT/LD Center programs, teachers use a similar process for integrating the arts.

Bright students who struggle in school need an appropriately differentiated program in order to be successful. Appropriate differentiation includes instructional adaptations and accommodations systematically provided to students (Maryland Task Force on Gifted and Talented Education, 1994; NAGC,

1998). Instruction and assignments should be structured in such a way that all students succeed to their fullest potential. Many resources for teachers detail appropriate adaptations and accommodations that obviate student's disabilities, allowing them to understand and present mastery of the material in a manner appropriate to their strengths. Utilizing appropriate assistive technology, which may include word processors, portable keyboards, electronic spellers, calculators, books on tape, and speech-to-text and text-to-speech software helps GT/LD students to succeed. Methodologies such as team teaching allow students to participate in GT classes while receiving the supports necessary for them to be successful.

The final component, which is crucial for ensuring that all other components are in place for these students, is comprehensive case management. The case manager, most often the special education resource teacher, must utilize the skills of a wide variety of professionals to build a team that includes students and parents. The case manager must communicate with all involved staff regarding the student's strengths and needs, as well as the appropriate adaptations and accommodations. The case manager must coordinate all aspects of the student's individual educational plan, making sure the student is both challenged and supported.

Strength-Based Instruction

Regardless of the program model used, instruction must be geared to a student's strengths, rather than his weaknesses. The utilization of a variety of adaptations, strategies, and accommodations that allow GT/LD students to access gifted instruction is widely advocated (Baum, 2004; Baum, Owen, & Dixon, 1991; Silverman, 1989; VanTassel-Baska, 1991). When a student's gifts are identified and nurtured, there is an increased willingness on the part of the student to put forth greater effort to complete tasks (Baum et al., 1989). Our experience has been that this focus on strengths works equally well for students who are gifted and have ADHD or autism spectrum disorders.

Working through a child's strengths puts a positive spin on learning, especially for a student who has had continued difficulty in school. Instruction, when it is differentiated, better matches an individual's abilities, styles, and needs. *Differentiation* is a way of thinking about and planning in order to meet the diverse needs of students based on their characteristics. Teachers differentiate content, process, and product according to students' readiness, interest, and learning profiles through a range of instructional and management strategies (Renzulli, 1977; Tomlinson, 1999).

Content is the subject matter prescribed by the state or district program of studies. For example, in social studies, students may be asked to write a research paper on the Civil War. *Process* is the internalization of information. Following the steps for the paper from notes, outline, and draft forms illustrates a process a student follows when dealing with the content material. *Product* is the outcome of the application of the processes to the content. The finished research paper is the product. Providing differentiation for these students, a variety of resources could be used to study the Civil War (content); organizational software and assisted note taking may aid in internalizing information (process); and the student may demonstrate her understanding through a model, dramatization, or PowerPoint® presentation (product) instead of a research paper.

The following are examples of different ways to support strength-based instruction (Tomlinson, 2000):

> *Working through a child's strengths puts a positive spin on learning, especially for a student who has had continued difficulty in school.*

- Study and practice models for gifted education (e.g., Creative Problem Solving, Bloom's Taxonomy)
- Provide activities that focus on students' individual gifts and interests
- Provide open-ended outlets for the demonstration of knowledge
- Use differentiated instruction
- Provide tasks that fit students' learning style
- Provide multisensory instruction
- Provide guided discovery, especially when introducing new topics

- Give student choices
- Use collaboratively designed rubrics
- Provide hands-on experiences
- Provide real-life tasks
- Integrate visual and performing arts
- Vary content

  ❖ Use multiple texts
  ❖ Use varied resources
  ❖ Compact curriculum
  ❖ Provide learning contracts

- Vary process

  ❖ Use interactive journals
  ❖ Use tiered assignments
  ❖ Create interest centers
  ❖ Create learning centers

- Vary product

  ❖ Provide varied modes of expression, materials, and technologies
  ❖ Require advanced assignments that require higher order thinking skills
  ❖ Provide authentic assessment
  ❖ Use evaluations by selves and others

Simultaneously, in order for students to obtain the greatest benefit from rigorous instruction, programming strategies must exist that provide additional support in the areas of weakness. In order to help students succeed, teachers must provide organizational strategies and allow alternatives to writing as a means of communication. It is also crucial that the instruction emphasize problem solving, reasoning, and critical thinking, as well as extending and elaborating the regular curriculum. Education of these children must focus on abstract ideas and generalizations (Baum et al., 1991). Differentiating rigorous instruction with appropriate individualized instructional adaptations and accommodations is necessary and requires close collaboration between special educators and general educators (Friend, 1996).

Adaptations and Accommodations

For twice-exceptional students who are gifted and have learning disabilities to effectively gain access to enriched and accelerated instruction, they often need to have appropriate adaptations and accommodations (Barton & Starnes, 1989; Baum, 1990; Cline & Schwartz, 1999; NAGC, 1998). Many accommodations allow bright students with learning challenges to demonstrate their knowledge without being hindered by the effects of their difficulties. In curricular planning, it is crucial that the teacher consider instructional methods and strategies that either circumvent the student's difficulties or build in the necessary scaffolding to empower him to be successful with the demands of the assignment. Again, this holds true not only for students with learning disabilities, but also for those with a wide range of learning difficulties, including autism spectrum disorders and ADHD.

Parents, when advocating for your child to receive adaptations and accommodations, it is essential to first understand the differences between an adaptation and an accommodation. An *adaptation* is a modification to the delivery of instruction or materials used, rather than a modification to the content being presented, as that can affect the fulfillment of curriculum goals (Lenz & Schumaker, 1999), while an *accommodation* is a procedure or enhancement that empowers a person with a disability to complete a task that he or she would otherwise be unable to complete because of his or her disability (Maryland State Department of Education, 1999).

Students often receive inadequate or inappropriate adaptations and accommodations, making their access to gifted instruction problematic (Weinfeld, Barnes-Robinson, Jeweler & Shevitz, 2002). It is natural for you, your child, and your child's teacher to have strong opinions and beliefs that influence which, if any, adaptations and accommodations you believe to be appropriate for your child. Some staff members will present you with a list of all possible accommodations to choose from as if it were a menu. Others may tell you which accommodations are appropriate based on their experience with other students who may or may not be like your child. You may feel that your child is entitled to every accommodation available, and that no one at school is looking out for his best interests. Or, you may believe that your child needs to be taught the basic skills just the way you were taught those skills years ago and that any accommodations are harmful.

In addition, some students believe that, because of their disability, they are entitled to have every accommodation possible, while other students reject the use of even the most reasonable accommodations because they think it might make them look different than their peers. Some staff members believe in providing any possible accommodation that will help a student do their best work, while other staff members think that many accommodations are unfair or harmful and are not preparing students for high-stakes exams, rigorous college courses, and the challenges of the real world. These differing beliefs and opinions often lead to either providing too few, too many, or the wrong accommodations.

Disagreement on the meaning and types of appropriate adaptations and accommodations for students is not only evident at the school level, but also at the state level. Although these policies relate to state regulations on formal assessments, they impact the accommodations that are allowed for classroom instruction and assessments. As teachers prepare their students for mandated state assessments, they often allow the same accommodations in their classroom instruction that will be allowed in the mandated assessments (Thurlow, House, Scott, & Ysseldyke, 2001).

Many accommodations allow students with disabilities to demonstrate their knowledge without being handicapped by the effects of their disabilities. Accommodations that are shown to be effective in research and practice are listed in this chapter's sections titled "What Works and What Doesn't Work" and "Overcoming Obstacles."

Review of research literature (see citations after each principle) revealed the following principles as the best practices for providing appropriate adaptations and accommodations for these students in order to ensure that access. Following each principle is a discussion of what we have found to be the merits of each guideline.

- *Accommodations used in assessments should parallel accommodations that are integrated into classroom instruction* (CEC, 2000; MSDE, 2000). During instruction and assessments, students should be allowed to access their strengths and truly demonstrate their knowledge. This is empowering, because the student is familiar and comfortable with the use of the accommodation. In addition, introducing an accommodation for testing only may actually hinder a student who is unfamiliar with the accommodation (Tindal & Fuchs, 1999).

- *The adaptations and accommodations should be aligned with the educational impact of the individual student's disability and with the student's needs as described in his or her IEP or 504 Plan* (CEC, 2000; MSDE, 2000). This principle relates to the idea of individualizing the accommodations for the specific student in question. Focusing on the individual student should answer the general educators' concern about whether the accommodation is needed by that student. The individual focus helps explain to the student what it is about their disability and needs that make it necessary for them to have the specific accommodations. Individualizing accommodations for the specific student in question is empowering, because it is consistent with what the individual student needs at that time.

- *The adaptations and accommodations should be based upon the strengths of the student* (Baum, 1990; Gardner, 1983; NAGC, 1998). Consistent with the idea that working through each individual's gifts is the most important method to use with these students, an accommodation will only be useful if it capitalizes on a gift, allowing a student to circumvent his difficulty. This is empowering, because it capitalizes on the individual's strengths.

- *Accommodations are based on what students need in order to be provided with an equal opportunity to show what they know without impediment of their disability* (Thurlow et al., 2001). This is consistent with the idea of leveling the playing field that appears frequently in research on learning-disabled students. Students should not be given an unfair advantage, but should be given an equal opportunity to succeed.

Although individual potential varies from student to student, all students should be provided with the opportunity to reach their greatest potential. This should answer an educator's objection about students being given an unfair advantage and should also answer the student's perception of receiving an unfair advantage. This is empowering, because students have a fair chance to demonstrate their abilities, rather than giving them a crutch when none is needed.

- *Assessments allow students, while using appropriate accommodations, to demonstrate their skills without the interference of their disabilities* (CEC, 2000). Throughout the research literature concerning GT/LD students, it is noted how important it is for all students to be included in assessments in order to give an accurate picture of how all students are performing. Assessments that allow students to demonstrate their knowledge are empowering.

- *After selecting and providing appropriate adaptations and accommodations, their impact on the performance of the individual student is evaluated and only those that are effective are continued* (Fuchs, Fuchs, Eaton, Hamlett, & Karns, 2000). Evaluation provides data for deciding which accommodations are useful and should be continued. The evaluation answers an educator's concerns about having too many or unnecessary accommodations. It should also assure you, the parents, that selected accommodations are of value. It further demonstrates to students that only effective accommodations are part of their individual plan. This is empowering, because only useful accommodations are continued.

- *The adaptations and accommodations should be reviewed, revised, and when appropriate, faded out over time, allowing the student to move from dependence to independence* (MSDE, 2000). Accommodations that are no longer needed are removed over time. You, your child, and your child's teacher will see progress and growth, which is empowering.

- *A multidisciplinary team, which considers the input of you and your child, decides upon the adaptations and accommodations* (IDEA, 1990; Section 504, 1975). Your input, and that of your child, is considered, which is empowering. The professionals make the final determination and do not abdicate their responsibility.

- *The appropriate adaptations and accommodations and the rationale for each of them are shared with all staff members who work with the student* (IDEA, 1990). This guideline will mitigate objections from general educators when they see the rationale for each accommodation. Your child will be empowered if you are in agreement with her teacher as to what she needs and is capable of doing at that time.

In summary, several key concepts emerge from these guidelines. The decisions regarding adaptations must be individualized for your child. The accommodations that are used in assessments must parallel those that are used in instruction and must be based on your student's strengths. The accommodations and assessments must provide an equal opportunity for your child to demonstrate her knowledge. And, lastly, accommodations must be evaluated often and only those that are effective should be continued.

When considering adaptations and accommodations, the overarching principle is to move your child, over time, from dependence to independence. With that in mind, an accommodation that is appropriate at a given point in time may be replaced at a later time with another accommodation that helps him to be more independent. For example, an appropriate accommodation for a student who lacks keyboarding skills, but is gifted verbally, may be to dictate a composition. Later, when the same student has learned keyboarding skills, the use of a word processor may be more appropriate because it moves him toward greater independence.

Finally, these guidelines include principles of effective decision making and implementation. While you and your child must have input into the process, the professionals must make the final decisions as to what is appropriate. There must be ongoing communication between the educators who are implementing these plans and yourself.

Social/Emotional Principles

The social/emotional needs of smart kids with learning difficulties are as important as the educational ones. With few exceptions, social and emotional issues can contribute to a child's lack of achievement. It is important to see whether negative behaviors and attitudes are the result of an inadequate program or personal issues. For some students, placement in an appropriate program that attends to their gifts and offers support for their learning needs will result in a positive turnaround in behavior and attitude. The development of skills and competencies in the social/emotional realm contribute to and complement the other best practices that promote success. Social/emotional health matters inside the classroom and beyond. Students, your child included, need tools and practice to develop self-efficacy, or the ability to know and to believe in one's self. They need tools and practice for becoming self-advocates, or the ability to know one's self and represent one's self with others. For example, the a GT/LD student needs to be able to approach a new teacher with necessary requests, such as, "I can speak, but I have trouble writing. Can I give you this report on tape?"

Students also need tools and practice to develop conflict resolution skills and communication skills. These are life skills that are essential for productive living. These are the skills that students need to help them make and keep friends, handle teasing, deal with anger and frustration, know when and how to ask for help, and get along with others at home and at school.

After students have had the opportunity to learn and practice the tool as it is applied to a problem situation, they are ready for lessons that teach the curriculum using the tool. These curricular connections between the real world and the academic world reinforce and expand the application of what the students have learned. The goal is that students see themselves as successful learners by knowing who they are, what they need, which tools work for them, and how to get what they need to succeed.

Interventions

Parents, when you or your child's teachers begin to suspect that she has learning difficulties, or even a specific learning disability such as dyslexia, the school should initiate a series of evaluation steps to determine if the learning problems exist and how best to accommodate for them. This section will discuss some of the evaluation steps schools should take to analyze and adapt for a student's learning problems.

When it is suspected that a bright or gifted student has learning challenges, it is crucial that the adults in his life meet with him to analyze his strengths and needs, and then together create an appropriate intervention plan. Creating this plan calls for analyzing a student's strengths, as well as his weaknesses. Next, the current program is evaluated to see how well it is nurturing and developing the student's strengths, while remediating, adapting, and accommodating for his weaknesses. Finally, recommendations are made for the program changes that will result in the appropriate level of challenge, and the instruction and support that will develop the student's gifts and strengthen his weaknesses.

> *When it is suspected that a bright or gifted student has learning challenges, it is crucial that the adults in his life meet with him to analyze his strengths and needs, and then together create an appropriate intervention plan.*

Analyzing a student's strengths calls for a careful examination of both formal and informal data from both the school and the community. District and statewide assessments, as well as individual assessments, can reveal evidence of outstanding achievement. These assessments may include intelligence tests, achievement tests, and other screening devices that may be employed by the school for admission to specific programs or special schools. Again, it is crucial to look at subtest scores, not just at the broad overall scores, to see patterns of strengths and needs in order to view students in the best possible light. School classes and activities where students have shown exceptional interest, perseverance, self-regulation, or outstanding achievement must be looked at carefully. Finally, it is crucial to look at reports of the student's performance in community activities, including those from private instructors, coaches, peers, and the student himself.

An analysis of a student's learning challenges comes from a close look at test scores and how the student performs in different academic areas. Typical stumbling blocks that prevent students' access to rigorous instruction often are found in the areas of writing, organization, reading, and memory. Again, district and statewide assessments, as well as individual assessments and screening devices can yield important information about specific learning challenges that individual students may be facing. A look at the student's school history, as well as his current functioning across different subject areas will provide further evidence of the specific challenges that he may face. Some students meet the criteria to be identified with a specific disability while others may not qualify for formal identification, but may still face significant challenges.

The final piece of analysis is to examine behavior and attention issues that may be preventing a student from succeeding in school. A thorough examination of these issues will look at performance across different subject areas at school, as well as performance at home and in the community. With this type of analysis, it will become evident which behaviors are a reaction to the current academic demands and which are more intrinsic to the student.

Once a student's strengths and challenges have been explored, schools should take a close look at their current program to see how well it is addressing both the identified strengths and challenges. Next, schools should explore the variety of supports, interventions, and instruction methods that are in place to both circumvent weaknesses and provide opportunities for strengthening them. In addition, schools must look at the special behavior management plans and counseling that are in place to meet the student's behavioral needs. Finally, the last step in the analysis is to look at the case management practices to ensure that all pieces are being addressed appropriately and that there is effective communication taking place between the school and a student's parents.

After completing a thorough analysis of the student's strength and weaknesses and the current instruction and interventions that are in place, school personnel will make recommendations about adjustments in the student's program. These recommendations become the intervention plan that helps each student reach his or her potential. Most importantly, the intervention plan recommends increased opportunities for students to nurture and develop their strengths. These opportunities range from differentiated instruction in the classroom, to participation in special projects and special classes or programs. As the obstacles are revealed in the analysis of student performance, adaptations and accommodations are built into the intervention plan that will allow the student to successfully access appropriate challenges. The intervention plan includes recommendations for the special instruction, behavioral/attention plans, and counseling support that the student needs to strengthen his weaker areas. The intervention plan specifies who is responsible for the case management and ensures that all staff and parents are functioning as a team to successfully implement the intervention plan. Finally, the intervention plan specifies how things will be implemented and who is responsible.

Bright students who have learning difficulties experience greater success when caring, involved adults and the student come together in a team approach to look at the student's strengths and needs. When his profile and his school's current program are carefully analyzed, interventions will be selected that will provide opportunities to develop the student's gifts, remove obstacles, and strengthen his areas of need.

Overcoming Obstacles

Smart kids with learning challenges often face stumbling blocks in the areas of writing, organization, reading, and memory. Possible stumbling blocks include:

- Writing, including:
  - ❖ the physical act of putting words on paper,
  - ❖ handwriting,
  - ❖ generating topics,
  - ❖ combining words into meaningful sentences,
  - ❖ organizing sentences and incorporating adequate details and support statements into organized paragraphs,
  - ❖ revising and editing, and
  - ❖ using language mechanics effectively (e.g., grammar, punctuation, spelling).

- Organization, including:
    - ❖ following multistep directions;
    - ❖ planning the steps needed to complete a task;
    - ❖ organizing desk, locker, notebook, and other materials;
    - ❖ locating needed materials;
    - ❖ breaking long-range assignments into manageable steps; and
    - ❖ prioritizing.

- Reading, including:
    - ❖ decoding unfamiliar words,
    - ❖ inferring meaning of new words,
    - ❖ summarizing,
    - ❖ reading fluently and quickly, and
    - ❖ using textbooks.

- Memory, including:
    - ❖ concentrating and keeping track of information,
    - ❖ quickly recalling details, and
    - ❖ retrieving details after time has passed.

Suggestions for appropriate adaptations and accommodations that work around student weaknesses related to these obstacles fall into four categories: assistive technology, instructional materials, teaching/assessment methods, and instruction. You may want to refer to the Bordering on Excellence tools on pp. 102–119 to efficiently and effectively differentiate content, process, and product in writing, organization, reading, and memory for these students. These materials provide specific suggestions for adaptations.

What Works and What Doesn't Work

The following is a comprehensive description of what strategies and methods work and don't work for GT/LD students (Weinfeld et al., 2002). While these strategies and methods were developed with GT/LD students in mind, they are appropriate for all smart kids with learning difficulties, including those with ADHD or autism spectrum disorders. This section encompasses social/emotional and academic recommendations, including specific strategies for each content area. Although the information is separated into different content areas, what works best for most of these students is an interdisciplinary approach. An interdisciplinary approach integrates thinking and learning skills and unifies content and process. This is important, because students learn best when provided with information in a variety of ways. Parents, you will want to look for signs of these effective practices in your child's classroom, and may want to share some of these practices with your child's teacher. Teachers of smart kids with learning difficulties can use these tips and suggestions to build a supportive environment for your students.

> *A strong classroom climate promotes its students' development of an understanding of their unique strengths, empowering them to successfully advocate for themselves.*

School Climate

Creating a comfortable, yet challenging classroom climate is essential. Addressing the social/emotional needs of smart kids with learning difficulties is critical to their achievement. The classroom climate should be designed to respect individuality, and accommodations should focus on strengths and potential for success, rather than remediation. A strong classroom climate promotes its students' development of an understanding of their unique strengths, empowering them to successfully advocate for themselves. Lowering standards, confrontational communication, and inflexible expectations that diminish student individuality is inappropriate in such a classroom. Instead, an ideal climate encourages interactive participation, flexibility, high standards, student participation in cooperative groups, individualized programming, active listening, and practice in conflict-resolution strategies.

The physical climate within the classroom should also be carefully orchestrated. A stimulating environment is ideal, with posters, collections, products, and highly visible student/teacher classroom standards and expectations for performance displayed throughout the room. Multimedia resources and technological tools, including word processors, tape recorders, calculators, and spell checkers should be available in a designated area in the classroom. In such an environment, students should have freedom of movement within the classroom. Careful attention must be given to both the physical and social climate in the classroom, creating an environment in which student needs are supported and abilities are recognized and nurtured.

Social/Emotional Skills and Strategies

At the beginning of the school year, teachers set the climate for collaboration, caring, respect, and negotiation for the year; good classrooms become a place where risk taking is encouraged and making mistakes is a way one grows and learns. The environment in such classrooms is not competitive, but rather a place where students measure their progress internally, and receive a sense of worth and accomplishment from within.

Classroom rules should be established by the students in a spirit of fairness and an appreciation and valuation of individual differences. The rules should be posted in a prominent place and always referred to when problems arise. Problem-solving processes need to be formally taught and practiced throughout the year, and students are expected to apply them as needed. Students should use these skills in their relationships in school, as well as be able to recognize when these skills are used in literature, history, and social studies. These skills have real-world applications and consequences. The problem-solving processes should be posted in prominent places for easy reference. Many classrooms have a suggestion box where students are encouraged to share ideas to improve the sense of community in the classroom, including suggestions for classroom rules and processes.

In every classroom, conflict is natural, always present, and better approached with skill training to help students deepen their understanding of self and others (Jeweler & Barnes-Robinson, 1999). Suggested tools for handling conflicts include:

- *Active listening*: a process for hearing what is being said and understanding the message being sent. Students are able to paraphrase back to the speaker the content and feelings of the message.

- *Triggers*: understanding the verbal and nonverbal actions that can stimulate confrontation and anger. Students learn how to assess situations that cause conflict in their lives to better understand their relationship to the conflict (based on a strategy originated by Judith A. Zimmer of Street Law, Inc.)
- *Questioning*: a strategy to acquire, clarify, and synthesize information. Student's appropriate use of questioning strategies encourages higher level thinking and promotes good discussion (McAlpine, Weincek, Jeweler, & Finkbinder, 1982).
- *Brainstorming*: a technique to generate new ideas about a thought or problem about something or with someone. Students learn a process to accept and consider all ideas, before learning to evaluate and prioritize them.

Role-playing can become an everyday strategy to practice how to talk with teachers, peers, and others in order to build and sustain positive relationships. When a problem arises in the classroom, on the playground, at the bus stop, or in the lunch room, all of the adults working with the students should take the time to process what has happened and utilize one of the problem-solving models that have been taught and practiced in the classroom. One example of a Creative Problem Solving model includes the following steps: recognize the problem, define the problem, gather ideas and data, rank ideas, test ideas, draw conclusions, and evaluate conclusions. (McAlpine et al., 1982).

Instructional Skills and Strategies

Gifted Instruction

Teachers, through training and self-study, can implement models for gifted education (e.g., Creative Problem Solving strategies and Bloom's Taxonomy) in their classrooms. Teachers should use activities that focus on their students' strengths and interests, allowing for self-directed choices, and teachers should implement instruction that is multisensory with hands-on experiences. Guided discovery (such as KWL charts asking a student what he knows, wants to learn, and did learn in a lesson) is a powerful strategy used especially well when introducing new topics. Support and clarification for embedded directions, both oral and written, should be given to students.

Integrating the visual and performing arts into the program has been proven to be an effective tool for gifted education. *Learning in and Through the Arts* (Burton, Horowitz, & Abeles, 1999) and *Champion of Change* (Fisk, 1999) studies found evidence that learning in the arts has significant effects on learning in other domains. Students are more motivated and teachers report that students retain information more readily when the arts are integrated into the curriculum.

Gifted teachers should recognize that implementing remedial instruction and rigid task guidelines are not successful practices for GT/LD students. They should also never believe that learning-disabled students could organize their thinking without accommodations or instruction. Good teachers do not consider a lack of production a sign of motivational weakness or lower intelligence. Rote memorization, forced oral reading, text-based instruction, and the use of only teacher-directed activities are not used in successful gifted classrooms. Instead, effective teachers use instruction that works around weaknesses, provides for production of alternative products, provides real-life tasks, provides open-ended outlets for the demonstration of knowledge, presents tasks that fit the student's learning style, differentiates instruction, and uses collaboratively designed rubrics.

Thinking Skills

Smart kids with learning difficulties are capable of exceptional thinking. Teachers should learn various thinking strategies, and teach, model, and practice these strategies in the classroom. Teachers should actively participate in the learning process using the Socratic method, a way of teaching using questions and answers that was practiced by the Greek philosopher, Socrates. This is a process that promotes discussion and responsibility. When this process in is place, students must come prepared for class, because they run the show. In turn, students learn to apply abstract concepts to everyday occurrences. Teachers can help students to transfer and apply the thinking strategies that work for them in their areas of strength to their areas of need. During the problem-solving process, teachers can use metacognitive skills and think aloud strategies to model the thinking process, or develop a thinking language to help students search for their own solutions. For example, a teacher may model a problem-solving process by posing an interesting problem and saying out loud what she is thinking as she solves the problem. Teachers should not assume that students already know thinking strategies and can apply them without ongoing practice.

Writing

Writing is often difficult for GT/LD students because many have trouble expressing themselves due to difficulty in organizing ideas, thoughts, and events, and giving attention to detail. Students also may have poor fine and gross motor skills. Teachers should focus on content more than handwriting skills, and the quality of the ideas expressed rather than the quantity.

Establishing the writing process through discussion and practice is an ongoing activity in gifted classrooms. Using assistive technology— portable word processors, computers, electronic spellers, organizational and word-predictive software—helps unlock a GT/LD student's ability to communicate what he knows and understands. Graphic organizers, mind mapping strategies, extended time for completion of work, and clear written expectations for writing tasks help students create good writing products. And, giving students prompts helps guide their purpose for writing. Rubrics, proofreading for one type of error at a time, and using a highlighter to indicate corrections aid in self-evaluation of written work. In addition, the publication of completed writing products for an audience serves as a great motivator during the writing process for smart kids with learning difficulties.

GT/LD students often have fine motor difficulties. Therefore, an occupational therapist should work with these students on handwriting instruction. The goal is legibility. Focusing on form, using mechanical pencils and grips, and using an appropriate handwriting program (e.g., Handwriting Without Tears [Olsen, 2002]) helps students who have difficulty writing by hand.

Lengthy handwriting tasks that result in fatigue and expectations that disregard a student's physical weakness or limitation are not effective methods for improving handwriting. Allowing students to use assistive technology including a word processor, word-predictive software, or speech-to-text software, is often an appropriate alternative to handwritten assignments.

Organization

Learning-disabled students frequently have problems with the organizational demands of assignments. Teachers can help minimize the impact of this problem by structuring assignments with very clear directions and steps. Good organizational practices include establishing specific due dates and time frames for long-term assignments, providing checkpoints for monitoring progress, providing time for students to organize their materials and assignments, and providing a specific location for students to place completed work. Teaching students effective organizational strategies helps students to become more self-sufficient learners. The supervised use of assistive technology and visual organizers, as well as the use of the more traditional supports such as assignment books, study guides, homework hotlines, and calendars, all help students become more organized. Promising new practices for improving student organization skills include posting homework assignments on Web pages, the use of hand-held organizers, and having students e-mail their own assignments to their home e-mail account.

Adults sometimes assume that students have the needed organizational skills, but are not using them because of laziness, lack of motivation, or poor attitudes. In the case of GT/LD students, this assumption is often not true, and such thinking can contribute to students' academic problems and low self-esteem.

Reading

Emphasis should be placed on comprehension of, listening for, and gaining pertinent information during reading instruction. Teachers must avoid focusing on word attack errors that do not affect comprehension. In addition, they should avoid using reading worksheets, round robin reading, and below-grade-level basal readers in their classrooms.

A successful reading program includes the use of literature for stimulating reading interest, oral discussion using supporting text, the development of expository reading, and the use of high-interest personal reading material that may be above grade level. Programs like the William and Mary Reading Program, created by the College of William and Mary, and the Junior Great Books program offer great opportunities for the development of reading and writing skills for students. These programs allow students to build on their abstract reasoning and comprehension skills. In addition to using these programs, students may also benefit from explicit instruction in phonological awareness, phonics, and decoding. The Wilson Reading Program is an excellent example of a program that has proven effective in teaching these reading skills. Accommodations such as books on tape or text-to-speech software (which enables students to scan any print material and have the computer read the material to them aloud) are also appropriate supports to reading instruction.

Memory

While students often possess outstanding abstract reasoning abilities and are able to see the big picture readily, they often have difficulty remembering and sequencing details. When teachers motivate students through the use of a variety of modalities, students are much more likely to remember the details. Students are more successful when they can utilize assistive technology, as well as a variety of supports in the classroom environment. Students become more independent in this area as they learn techniques to enhance their own memory, such as mnemonics, visual imagery, outlining, note taking, and highlighting. Other successful strategies include having students sequence activities after a lesson or event, having students teach information to other students, providing students with environmental cues and prompts, relating information presented to the student's previous experiences, and telling them what to listen for when given directions or information.

Teaching in a way that requires students to recall details, which are presented in a context that is not meaningful or does not incorporate a variety of modalities, is not beneficial for these students. Once again, it is important not to assume that although these students have great ability in certain areas, they have learned the needed skills to circumvent their difficulties with memory of details.

Evaluation/Assessment

Students and teachers should collaborate on the type of evaluations and assessment methods and tools that will give an accurate picture of student understanding of both content and process material. Evaluations are based on instruction and reflect the attainment of the key concepts and basic understandings that are the focus of the curriculum.

Providing objectives, study guides, vocabulary, memory strategies, rubrics, and support and clarification for embedded questions aid students in accurately sharing what they know. Models of appropriate responses to prompts are helpful for students to use as a guide for creating their own responses. Differentiation in evaluations and assessments is important, because evaluations must allow students to demonstrate their skills without the interference of their weaknesses. Accommodations to more traditional assessments include audiotaping responses, using a graphic organizer in lieu of paragraph responses, creating a model, or giving a speech.

Evaluations and assessments should be designed to maximize the student's demonstration of her knowledge of concepts and content. Lengthy essays, penalties for spelling in content areas, time limits, and matching tasks may not communicate a student's understanding of course material clearly. Attention should also be given to the formatting of evaluations in order to circumvent visual processing difficulties.

The following sections present subject specific examples that illustrate how to apply instructional skills and strategies in content areas.

Mathematics

Preassessment of student mastery of mathematical categories (e.g., decimal fractions, whole numbers, statistics, and probability) and objectives is an appropriate place to begin instruction. Focusing on developing conceptual skills and problem-solving strategies is essential, because these students are capable of higher order thinking (Bloom, Englehart, Furst, Hill, & Krathwohl, 1956). Once they have learned a concept, they will be able to apply it to a novel problem or situation. Using interactive, hands-on programs (e.g., Hands-on Equations), manipulatives, and math tools help students grasp content and concepts. Students may need untimed tests, a reduction in the number of problems, and direct instruction in the use of calculators for accommodations to be successful.

Giving lengthy, repetitive assignments; having students copy from textbooks, overheads, or blackboards; or a focus on computation alone are not effective instructional strategies for smart kids with learning difficulties. Appropriate accommodations, such as a calculator, allow these students to utilize their often-superior math reasoning abilities while not being held back by their computation skills. For example, a student may be capable of mastering advanced math concepts, like algebraic equations, but can't remember how to do basic computations, like simple division. When given a calculator to use for the basic computations, the problem is eliminated.

Science

Science instruction that offers hands-on, interactive experiences is most successful because it involves students in the learning process, utilizing their strengths while working around their weaknesses in reading or writing. Activities that incorporate problem solving and real-life investigations with a purpose and an end product, along with a thematic approach that allows for students to direct their search for knowledge and answers, are meaningful to students because they are relevant and generated by the students themselves. Simulations and the integration of the visual and the performing arts are extremely successful when teaching science content and concepts.

What Needs to Be Done for Smart Kids With Learning Difficulties and Who Is Responsible?

85

Memorization of facts and emphasis on reading and writing are often counterproductive science activities for GT/LD students. The students may become experts in specific areas of interest when enough time is provided for them to do research projects. The acquisition of expertise through independent study enables these students to become valuable contributors to cooperative group projects. When researching a topic, the use of writing strategies is crucial for these students.

Social Studies

Social studies instruction is based on learning multiple facts and processing that content appropriately. Students should be responsible for learning the historical, economic, political, geographic, and cultural content standards. Students should be expected to construct understandings through systems of processing information, critical thinking, and problem solving. Thematic units, simulations, hands-on activities and projects, the use of various forms of media, integration of the visual and the performing arts, and extension or enrichment activities help GT/LD students learn the necessary social studies concepts. Instruction led by textbook reading and focusing on memorization of facts, rather than understanding the concepts, is not an effective learning strategy for these students. For example, a student may not be able to write about ancient Greece but can participate in a simulation of the political processes of ancient Greece to demonstrate his understanding.

Roles and Responsibilities

The following is an analysis of the roles and responsibilities of those involved in the education of smart kids with learning difficulties.

Administrator/Principal

The school administrator must create a school climate that fosters respect for individuals and ideas, innovation, and openness to differing learning styles and teaching methodologies required to reach these students. The administrator should provide ongoing explanations to school staff, parents, and community members about programs and services for gifted/learning-disabled students. The administrator should model a collaborative approach for discipline that empowers students and teaches them to use conflict resolution and Creative Problem Solving strategies. By using a conflict resolution model, students have the opportunity to employ their excellent cognitive skills while simultaneously developing their intrapersonal and interpersonal skills.

The principal, as the instructional leader, should know every student in the building and offer support to the teachers in meeting the needs of each student. Interventions include allocating appropriate support staff; creating scheduling options; ordering appropriate materials and resources, including technology; and providing guidance for the creation and utilization of appropriate adaptations and accommodations for students. The administrator is also responsible for coordinating meetings to plan for implementing both gifted instruction and special education instruction that will enable each student to succeed to his or her fullest potential. The administrator also coordinates the required IEP or 504 team process for identified gifted students with disabilities and ensures the implementation of their individualized educational plans. The principal must make sure that the best practices for educating all bright kids with learning challenges occurs. He or she also monitors the inclusion of learning-disabled students in all school events so that they are an integral part of the school community.

General Educator

The general education classroom teacher needs to recognize and accept that these students are gifted first and disabled second, and to understand that they need to be viewed primarily in terms of their giftedness. Therefore, the program in general education classrooms should focus on developing and utilizing the strengths of the student—not only on remediating weaknesses. Teachers should provide strategies that circumvent students' deficits, empowering these students to participate in the same rigorous curriculum as other gifted children. As a result, students are immersed in a climate that promotes self-efficacy and a solid sense of self-sufficiency, while being provided with instruction that demands the use of their gifted abilities.

The general educator can nurture giftedness in numerous ways. He or she can provide necessary accommodations for these students while ensuring the appropriate level of acceleration and enrichment by differentiating instruction throughout its content, process, and product expectations. Teachers must allow students to see the big picture and state objectives clearly so that students know what is expected. Students are exposed to advanced materials and concepts that require them to make connections and extensions to knowledge previously obtained. Within the advanced content, teachers should have students go beyond the factual information to analyze, interpret, evaluate, create, and make connections. Teachers should compact the curriculum to free up time for advanced levels of instruction. The use of simulations and open-ended questions also provide students with opportunities to engage in higher level thinking skills. Students are taught strategies to circumvent deficits. One example is using a mnemonic device (such as HOMES for the Great Lakes: Huron, Ontario, Michigan, Erie, Superior) to help for memory issues. In addition, technological equipment should be made available in general education classes to accommodate a student's needs.

Teachers should encourage students to take responsibility and ownership for the decisions made about their education. In completing tasks and assignments, students are provided with choices to demonstrate their knowledge and understanding of concepts and content. By maintaining high expectations and standards in an atmosphere of support, humor, and comfort, teachers help students grow academically and love learning.

The general educator also keeps the lines of communication open between students, staff, and parents and guardians. When all parties work respectfully to establish open and direct communication, a lasting partnership is possible.

Special Educators

Special education resource teachers, speech and language teachers, occupational therapists, instructional aides, and all staff working with the student with disabilities are part of the team of school professionals responsible for learning-disabled students receiving needed services.

The resource teacher acts as a case manager, monitoring the program, accommodations, and progress of the student. He or she also teaches the student strategies and skills he needs to access gifted instruction. These may include using reading, writing, organization, and memory aids, as well as self-advocacy skills and other social skills. Through direct instruction, the resource teacher teaches the strategies to develop skills that remedy the academic problems affected by the student's disability. For many students with disabilities, their only special education intervention consists of one class period each day with the resource teacher. The special education resource teacher not only works with students with disabilities but also works with the school's staff to help them develop an understanding of how to meet the instructional needs of learning-disabled children while not reducing intellectual expectations. The special education resource teacher also maintains ongoing communication with parents.

School Counselor

The school counselor plays a vital, multifaceted role in helping to provide an enriching, nurturing, and supportive school climate for these students. By the time these children are correctly identified and an appropriate learning environment is provided, they have often experienced failure, both academically and socially. The counselor helps students develop an accurate understanding of their strengths and needs. These students are bright and perceptive, and can see through interventions that are not genuine and respectful. An environment where they experience success and are surrounded by people who value them for who they are is essential for their continued success.

The counselor supports the program by coordinating and sharing information with the school "team" to help them understand the unique characteristics of the students. Information is shared through in-service sessions, team meetings, individual meetings, and meetings with the principal. The counselor works with staff to ensure that appropriate adaptations and accommodations are made for students and that the child's individual program is well-coordinated. There is a danger that smart kids with learning difficulties will have either their giftedness or their areas of need addressed in isolation. The challenge is to simultaneously serve these kids in both dimensions. In addition, the counselor helps the staff clarify the rules and expectations for each setting the student will likely encounter.

The counselor meets with students with disabilities individually, in small groups, in the whole class, and in informal settings regarding issues and concerns. The counselor meets with students who come to see her on their own accord, as well as those who come at the suggestion of a parent or teacher. Sometimes, counselors conduct class meetings and give social skills training to students that includes topics like dealing with disappointments, coping strategies, making and keeping friends, clarifying rules and expectations, risk taking in social settings, and asking for help. The counselor helps students to develop a full understanding of their unique strengths and needs. This sets the stage for students to learn which adaptations and accommodations are effective for them, allowing them to become self-advocates. The counselor becomes an advocate for the student when the student feels he or she cannot fend for him- or herself. The counselor should also encourage students to participate in school clubs, activities, teams, and organizations. Counseling interventions often set the tone for the school's positive acceptance of bright underachieving kids, including gifted students with disabilities.

The counselor's role also includes communicating with you, the parents of these students, individually and participating in parenting groups. Through participation in a partnership, counselors can help you learn to accept and value your children for who they are, and will more than likely encourage you to become involved with organizations that serve and represent your learning-disabled child.

Mentors

A well-designed mentor program can offer an optimum match and an ideal climate for bright students with learning challenges, by providing an opportunity to focus on the students' strengths and potential for success, rather than their lack of achievement in specific areas. Mentors who are sensitive to the students' needs and who offer positive reinforcement of the students' efforts and accomplishments are able to help them realize their creative and intellectual potential.

Two of the most important components of a successful mentor program are the one-on-one mentor to student relationship and the opportunity to pursue an area of interest to the student. Many of the learning problems that manifest themselves in the regular classroom are not apparent when working one-on-one with a mentor. Poor organizational skills and little follow-through are minimized when the student is working with a mentor who is able to provide the needed guidance and support to be successful. In addition, it has been shown that students show strong task commitment when the topic is personally meaningful (Baum, 1984; Baum et al., 1991; Whitmore, 1980). Therefore, motivation is increased when a mentor program provides the student with the opportunity to select a topic of interest. In addition, the mentor serves to validate the students as learners, increasing their self-concept. In the regular classroom, many assignments require large amounts of reading and writing, areas that often cause difficulty for these students. A mentor program that is designed to allow for alternative products enables students to gain awareness of their capabilities and learning styles.

Mentors must be carefully screened and selected based on their knowledge in a specific field and their eagerness to share their skills with young people. Through the unique one-to-one relationship, the mentors are able to help the students pursue a passion, while guiding them in developing skills necessary to succeed in school. For some students, the mentor program is the only programming necessary in order for the student to be provided the boost that he or she needs to gain confidence and be successful. (For a description of a successful mentor program, see Chapter 4.)

Students

Your child needs to be empowered as he becomes involved in his learning. Once provided with tools, strategies, and skills for learning, your child can successfully develop and use his intellect. Students have responsibilities as learners. In order to be successful, your child must recognize and accept both his strengths and needs and gain an understanding of how he learns best (metacognition). Once aware of his specific issues, he can become active in learning and practicing strategies for thinking, organization, communication, problem solving, and the use of technology. Students are expected to eventually complete assignments independently, become self-directed, and seek help and support as needed. Learning and practicing strategies for developing self-efficacy (the belief in self) and self-advocacy (the ability to tell others what is needed) make it possible for these students to become risk takers and lifelong learners. Over time, students develop the skills and maturity that allow them to become partners in making decisions regarding their Individualized Educational Plans.

Parents/Guardian

Parents, you are usually the most active advocates for smart kids with learning difficulties. Children are often identified as gifted or as gifted/learning disabled because their parents or guardians have noticed the gifts of their children in their home environment. Parents, you should become teammates along with your child and the education professionals at his school in creating a successful learning experience for him.

You can support your child's success in school in a number of ways. You should maintain an open attitude toward instruction and school and help your child realize that school is his job and a gateway to life achievement. You know your child's strengths and needs and should help your child to understand them. You must also help your child understand

> *In order to be successful, your child must recognize and accept both her strengths and needs and gain an understanding of how she learns best.*

and actively attempt to meet her goals, including those in the IEP, 504 Plan, and less formal plans.

You should communicate with your student and the school staff on a variety of issues, including progress and planning. You can help your child focus on school assignments and, at the same time, empower your student to accept responsibility for his own learning. You can transfer strong advocacy skills to your children and reinforce thinking and leadership skills learned at school. You may be able to facilitate communication between school staff and other personnel in the community, such as doctors, therapists, and tutors who may be working with your child. You should also implement suggestions for parenting techniques that foster the development of self-esteem and self-efficacy to provide consistency and continuity between a child's home and school experiences.

> *Parents, you should become teammates along with your child and the education professionals at his school in creating a successful learning experience for him.*

TIPS and Tools: Supplementary Materials

Included in this section:

- What Works/What Doesn't Work Charts
- Bordering on Excellence Tools
- Who's Who: Roles and Responsibilities

What Works/What Doesn't Work Charts

The following are charts of what works and what doesn't work for bright kids with learning difficulties.

<table>
<tr><td>

TIPS

Teacher:
Use as a self-evaluation checklist. Use charts when planning for instruction. Use as a communication tool with parents, other staff members, and students.

Parent:
Use as an evaluation tool of your child's school experience. Use it for creating questions to ask at conferences. Work with your child to implement what works and what doesn't work regarding homework.

Student:
Ask your teacher and parent about what works and what doesn't work for you. Use the chart information when practicing self-advocacy skills.

</td></tr>
</table>

What Works/What Doesn't Work Charts

Area of Concern	What Works	What Doesn't Work
Climate	• Understanding of student's unique strengths and needs • Promoting self-advocacy skills • Comfortable, yet challenging classroom with a stimulating environment—posters, collections, and products displayed • Highly visible class standards and expectations • Student freedom of movement within classroom • Interactive participation • Flexibility • High classroom standards • Cooperative groups • Individualized programing • Conflict resolution instruction • Multimedia resources available • Technological tools available—word processors, calculators, spell checkers	• Routine and remedial drill and practice with focus on students' disabilities • Lowering standards • Confrontational communication • Inflexible expectations that diminish student individuality
Social/Emotional	• Respecting students • Encouragement • Connecting to students through their strengths and interests • Focusing on strengths, analyzing successes, and applying strengths to weaknesses • Teaching conflict resolution skills • Teaching self-advocacy and self-efficacy • Offering choices	• Disrespect • Sarcasm • Limiting options and choices • Stressing the importance of the weaknesses • Using negative consequences only • Using one instructional method • Denying access to positive learning experiences • Discipline as punishment only

Area of Concern	What Works	What Doesn't Work
Social/Emotional, continued	• Offering alternative ideas and options • Extracurricular enrichment activities • Teaching students to channel frustrations • Easing and removing barriers and planning for the future • Using nonverbal strategies to support students • Discipline as a teachable moment • Encouraging risk taking • Opportunities to practice skills to build confidence	• Lack of communication • Fear of being wrong or making mistakes
Gifted Instruction	• Studying, knowing, and practicing models for gifted education • Activities that focus on students' gifts and interests • Open-ended outlets for the demonstration of knowledge • Differentiated instruction • Tasks that fit student's learning styles • Multisensory instruction • Support and clarification for directions • Offering students choices • Alternative product options • Collaboratively designed rubrics • Hands-on experiences • Real-life tasks • Integration of visual and performing arts	• Remedial instruction • Rigid task guidelines • Belief that GT/LD students can organize their thinking without accommodations or instruction • Perceiving lack of production as a sign of motivational weakness or lower intelligence • Rote memorization • Forced oral reading • Text-based instruction • Only teacher-directed activities (lecture only; activities that do not encourage student decision making or participation)

Area of Concern	What Works	What Doesn't Work
Thinking	• Teachers learning thinking strategies • Teaching and modeling thinking strategies • Practicing thinking strategies in the classroom • Applying thinking strategies • Working with GT/LD students to formulate questions, think through problems, use the Socratic method, actively participate in the learning process, apply abstract concepts to everyday occurrences, develop a thinking process, develop a thinking language, or search for their own solutions • Utilizing metacognitive skills • Transferring/applying thinking strategies that work in areas of strengths to areas of need	• Assuming students know thinking strategies • Assuming students can apply thinking strategies without ongoing practice
Reading	• Emphasis on comprehension, and gaining information • Using literature for stimulating reading interests • High-interest personal reading material • Programs like the William and Mary Reading Program that build abstract reasoning and comprehension skills • Development of expository reading • Oral discussion using supporting text • Explicit instruction in phonological awareness, phonics, and decoding (such as that used in Wilson Reading Program) • Using books on tape and speech-to-text software	• Focusing on errors that do not affect comprehension • Reading worksheets • Round-robin reading • Categorizing below-grade-level basal readers

Area of Concern	What Works	What Doesn't Work
Writing	• Establishing writing process through ongoing discussion and practice • Assistive technology—portable word processors, computers, electronic spellers, word-predictive software • Graphic organizers • Mind mapping strategies • Extended time for completion of work • Clearly written expectations for writing tasks • Writing prompts • Proofreading for one type of error at a time • Highlighters to indicate corrections • Publication of writing for an audience	• Focusing on handwriting instead of content • Quantity versus quality • Using red pens to denote errors
Organization	• Electronic organizers • Software organization programs • Study guides that help locate information and answers • Assignment books and calendars for recording assignments • Graphic organizers—outlines, webs, diagrams, storyboards • Establishing specific due dates for short assignments and time frames for long-term assignments • Breaking up tasks into workable and obtainable steps • Providing checkpoints for long-term assignments and monitoring progress frequently • Providing time to organize materials and assignments.	• Assuming students have the needed organizational skills • Attributing poor organizational skills to lack of motivation, bad attitude, or laziness • Assigning long-term or complicated assignments without supports for organization • Expecting students to utilize organizational supports without providing instruction in the use of those supports

Area of Concern	What Works	What Doesn't Work
Organization, continued	• Providing a homework hotline or Web page • A specific location for students to place completed work • Monitoring students' accuracy in recording assignments and/or providing printed copy. • Multiple modalities when presenting directions, explanations, and instructional content • Having students sequence activities after a lesson or event	
Memory	• Providing students with a copy of the information that highlights key facts • Having students tape record directions or information • Providing students with environmental cues and prompts—posted rules, steps for performing tasks, etc. • Allowing students to use resources in the environment to recall information—notes, textbooks, pictures, etc. • Relating information to student's previous experiences • Having students outline, highlight, underline, or summarize information that should be remembered • Telling students what to listen for when being given directions or receiving information • Associative cues or mnemonic devices • Teaching visual imagery	• Using only one modality, such as a lecture, to teach a lesson • Expecting students to recall facts without support • Expecting students to utilize mnemonics, visual imagery, technology, or other supports without teaching them how to use these tools

Area of Concern	What Works	What Doesn't Work
Handwriting	• Focusing on form • Mechanical pencils or grips • Appropriate handwriting program • Assistive technology	• Lengthy handwriting tasks that result in fatigue • Expectations that disregard students' physical weaknesses or limitations
Evaluations and Assessments	• Student/teacher collaboration on the evaluation and assessment methods and tools • Evaluations based on instruction reflecting the key concepts and basic understandings of the curriculum • Providing objectives, study guides, vocabulary, acceptable responses, support, and clarification for questions • Differentiation • Audiotape responses • Graphic organizers in lieu of paragraph responses • Creating a model • Giving a speech	• Lengthy essays • Penalties for spelling in content areas • Time limits • Matching tasks

Note. Adapted fom unpublished charts by Larry March and Martha Abolins. Reprinted with permission.

Bordering on Excellence Tools

The Bordering on Excellence tools drive theory to practice by combining the best practices and guiding principles for appropriate adaptations and accommodations with successful strategies to help teachers tailor instruction for each student.

They interface with any instructional material and will allow educators to consider the multiple issues that they need to effectively and efficiently address when differentiating content, process, and product.

The components are:

- *Frame of Reference:* This is a desk and/or notebook reference companion designed to address the differentiated needs and expertise of staff. It is useful for training and teacher/parent conferences. It includes three sections: The Big Picture, Possible Stumbling Blocks, and Adaptations and Accommodations for Overcoming Obstacles. Simply reproduce or copy the pages that follow into a format that suits you best, whether it is several two-sided cards or a packet of information.
- *Bordering on Excellence Frame:* A blank frame that provides an alternative format for analyzing either the needs of specific students or evaluating the obstacles inherent in a lesson. It is useful for training and teacher/parent conferences. We have provided examples for you to follow, along with blank frames for each of the four trouble areas faced by smart kids with learning difficulties. These frames can also be used to evaluate instructional materials, including curricular guides, books, teacher-made study guides, and workbooks.

TIPS

Teacher:
Use the collection of tools as references, for planning purposes, as a student record form, with instructional materials to obviate student weaknesses and tap into strengths, and as a communication tool with parents, other staff members, and students.

Parent:
Use with teacher and child when working on homework. Use as a basis for discussion at teacher conferences and meetings.

Student:
Keep in your notebook as a reference. Work with your teacher and parent to ease difficulties with materials.

Bordering on Excellence Frame of Reference

The Big Picture

ENSURE

- Focus on strengths and interests
- Instructional adaptations and accommodations
- Comprehensive case management

TEACH

- Decoding skills
- Writing process
- Language conventions (e.g., spelling, grammar, punctuation, usage)
- Note taking
- Highlighting
- Outlining
- Summarizing
- Prioritizing tasks
- Organizing materials
- Keyboarding
- Word processing

PROVIDE

- Acceleration and enrichment
- Open-ended tasks
- Real-life applications
- Realistic simulations
- Emphasis on problem solving, reasoning, and critical thinking
- Opportunities for student choice
- Alternative product options
- Integration of the arts
- Approach that teaches to various learning styles
- Opportunities to create authentic products
- Multisensory approach to learning
- Flexibility in classroom organization

Possible Stumbling Blocks

WRITING
- the physical act of putting words on paper
- handwriting
- generating topics
- combining words into meaningful sentences
- organizing sentences and incorporating adequate details and support statements into organized paragraphs
- revising and editing
- using language mechanics effectively (e.g., grammar, punctuation, spelling)

ORGANIZATION
- following multistep directions
- planning the steps needed to complete a task
- organizing desk, locker, notebook, and other materials
- locating needed materials
- breaking long-range assignments into manageable steps
- prioritizing

READING
- decoding unfamiliar words
- inferring meaning of new words
- summarizing
- reading fluently and quickly
- using textbooks

MEMORY
- concentrating and keeping track of information
- quickly recalling details
- retrieving details after time has passed

Adaptations and Accommodations—Writing

ASSISTIVE TECHNOLOGY	INSTRUCTION MATERIALS	TEACHING/ASSESSMENT	INSTRUCT STUDENTS IN:
• voice recognition software • writing organizational software • electronic spellers and dictionaries • computer with spelling and grammar checker • portable keyboards • word prediction software • programs that read writing aloud, providing for audio spell checker, proofreading, word prediction, and homophone distinction • tape recorder for transcription after student dictation	• step-by-step written directions • a proofreading checklist • graphic organizers • scoring rubric, models, and anchor papers for students to evaluate work • guides such as story starters, webs, and outlines • dictionaries, word banks, and thesauri • personal dictionaries of misused and misspelled words • highlighters to indicate errors and corrections • copy of teacher's notes or of another student's notes (NCR paper) • pencil grips and mechanical pencils • paper with raised lines • slant boards	• focus on content rather than mechanics • focus on quality rather than quantity • prepare storyboards, guided imagery, dramatization, or projects before the writing process • set important purposes for writing, such as writing for publication • allow students to write in areas of interest or expertise • allow students to show understanding through alternative products • reduce or alter written requirements • break down assignments into smaller, manageable parts • allow additional time • proofread for one type of error at a time	• the writing process • prewriting strategies, including brainstorming, making a web, and drawing about the topic • rewriting questions into answer form • writing for a variety of purposes • combining words into meaningful sentences • formulating topic sentences • organizing sentences and incorporating adequate details and support statements into paragraphs • language conventions (e.g., grammar, punctuation, spelling, usage) • history/structure of language • keyboarding skills

Adaptations and Accommodations—Writing, continued

TEACHING/ASSESSMENT		
• permit work with partners or small groups during revising, editing, and proofreading		
• permit students to use words or phrases instead of complete sentences		
• allow students to make artistic (visual, spatial, and performing) products		
• allow students to make scientific and technological products		
• provide dictated response		
• students review and summarize important information and directions		
• invite student questions regarding directions and assignments		
• provide a portfolio assessment of products and performances		
• allow alternative spelling		
• provide students with a list of needed materials and their locations		

Adaptations and Accommodations—Organization

ASSISTIVE TECHNOLOGY	INSTRUCTION MATERIALS	TEACHING/ASSESSMENT	INSTRUCT STUDENTS IN:
• electronic organizers • software organization programs • audiotaping assignments • e-mailing assignments from school to student's home account	• visual models, storyboards, Venn diagrams, matrices, and flow charts • study guides that help locate information and answers • highlighters, index tabs, and colored stickers • assignment books and calendars for recording assignments • outlines, webs, diagrams, and other graphic organizers	• use short, simple directions • provide advanced organizers regarding what students will know by the end of the lesson • post class and homework assignments in the same area each day and assure that students record them and/or have a printed copy • verbally review class and home-work assignments • list and verbally review step-by-step directions for assignments • work with students to establish specific due dates for short assignments and time frames for long-term assignments • break up tasks into workable and obtainable steps • encourage study buddies • give examples and specific steps to accomplish tasks	• how to prioritize tasks • how to ask questions regarding unclear directions and assignments • metacognition • how to break long-term assignments into manageable components • note taking • a routine to follow to prepare for each class • a system for organizing note-books and lockers • how to use software organization programs • how to use assignment books, calendars, electronic organizers, visual models, and graphic organizers • how to access homework help

Adaptations and Accommodations—Organization, continued

ASSISTIVE TECHNOLOGY	INSTRUCTION MATERIALS	TEACHING/ASSESSMENT	INSTRUCT STUDENTS IN:
		• provide checkpoints for long-term assignments and monitor progress frequently • students review and summarize important information and directions • invite student questions regarding directions and assignments • provide students with a list of needed materials and their locations • periodically check notebooks and lockers • provide homework hotline or structured homework assistance • post a daily routine and explain any changes in that routine • provide an uncluttered work area • label and store materials in designated locations • provide a specific location for students to place completed work • provide samples of finished products	

Adaptations and Accommodations—Reading

ASSISTIVE TECHNOLOGY	INSTRUCTION MATERIALS	TEACHING/ASSESSMENT	INSTRUCT STUDENTS IN:
• CD-ROMs with audio component • electronic spellers that speak words aloud • books on tape and digital books • computer programs that allow words to be read aloud • text-to-speech software	• interviews, speakers, and demonstrations • multimedia presentations • tape recorded directions or tests • text study guides and graphic organizers to help locate information • access to challenging reading programs, like Junior Great Books • high-interest, appropriate-level reading material and multilevel texts about the same topic • above–grade-level high-interest reading material • rich literature experiences • expository reading experiences • visuals (outlines, graphic organizers, charts, photographs, diagrams, and maps) to help students understand written information • word banks	• develop interest and curiosity by activating prior knowledge • use a multiple intelligence approach • begin with an experience or project • teach through the arts (drama, visual arts, poetry) • utilize simulations and moral dilemmas • encourage reading related to students' areas of interest • set purposes for reading and state what students should know after reading the text • ask lower level comprehension questions in order to build up to higher level questions • cue students to important words and concepts verbally and through highlighting • teach vocabulary in context	• phonological awareness and phonics • a multisensory reading approach • a rule-based approach to reading • sight vocabulary• prefixes and suffixes • how to use a textbook (i.e., understanding the index, table of contents, glossary, charts, tables, captions, and bold text) • outlining and note taking

Adaptations and Accommodations—Reading, continued

ASSISTIVE TECHNOLOGY	INSTRUCTION MATERIALS	TEACHING/ASSESSMENT	INSTRUCT STUDENTS IN:
		• give students the opportunity to read silently before reading aloud • allow students to choose whether or not to read aloud • pair students who have strong decoding skills with weak decoders • allow students to do difficult tasks in small groups • read directions or tests aloud • allow additional time for reading • teach students to outline, underline, or highlight important points • encourage students to take notes while reading • offer support and clarification for imbedded directions in text	

Adaptations and Accommodations—Memory

ASSISTIVE TECHNOLOGY	INSTRUCTION MATERIALS	TEACHING/ASSESSMENT	INSTRUCT STUDENTS IN:
• software programs as an alternative way of presenting information • tape recording directions or information • software programs to organize key points	• multiple modalities when presenting directions, explanations, and instructional content • those that address multiple learning styles • utilize materials that are meaningful to students • copies of the information that highlight key facts	• have students repeat the directions or information back to teacher • have students repeat information to selves • have students recall important details at the end of a lesson • have students sequence activities after a lesson or event • have students teach information to other students • have students deliver the schedule of events to other students • deliver directions, explanations, and instructional content in a clear manner and at an appropriate pace • provide students with a written list of materials and directions • give auditory and visual cues to help students recall information	• transforming information from one modality to another (e.g., from verbal to a diagram or from visual to verbal) • questioning any directions, explanations, and instructions they do not understand • delivering increasingly long verbal messages • how to organize information into smaller units • using environmental sources in the environment to recall information (e.g., notes, pictures) • how to practice memory skills by engaging in activities that are purposeful, such as delivering messages or being in charge of a task • how to highlight and summarize information

Adaptations and Accommodations—Memory, continued

ASSISTIVE TECHNOLOGY	INSTRUCTION MATERIALS	TEACHING/ASSESSMENT	INSTRUCT STUDENTS IN:
		• provide students with environmental cues and prompts such as posted rules and steps for performing tasks • have students use resources in the environment to recall information (e.g., notes, textbooks, pictures, etc.) • relate information presented to students' previous experiences • have students outline, highlight, underline, or summarize information that should be remembered • repeat information by using different experiences and modalities • provide students with information from a variety of sources • use visual imagery • tell students what to listen for when receiving information	• practicing repetition of information • engaging in memory games and activities • listening skills • visual imagery • systematic ways to store and retrieve information • how to use advanced organizers, such as lists, tables, and graphics • study and test-taking skills • routines for beginning a task • how to recognize key words

Bordering on Excellence Frame Example

Adaptations/Accommodations
WRITING
Possible Stumbling Blocks

- the physical act of putting words on paper
- handwriting
- generating topics
- formulating topic sentences
- combining words into meaningful sentences
- using language mechanics effectively (e.g., grammar, punctuation, spelling)
- organizing sentences and incorporating adequate details and support statements into organized paragraphs
- revising and editing

Instructional Materials

- step-by-step written directions
- a proofreading checklist
- scoring rubrics, models, and anchor papers for students to evaluate their own work
- graphic organizers
- guides such as story starters, webs, story charts, outlines
- dictionaries, word banks, and thesauri
- personal dictionaries of misused and misspelled words
- highlighter to indicate errors/corrections
- copy of teacher notes or of another student's notes (NCR paper)
- pencil grips
- paper with raised lines
- mechanical pencils
- slant board

NOTES:

−*5 students with difficulties in writing*

−*written production required*
  - *literature webs (2 chapters)*
  - *vocabulary webs (2 words)*
  - *change matrix with specific evidence*
  - *written reflections*

−*I will need to address the following:*
  - *stumbling blocks (circled)*
  - *interventions (circled)*
  - *technology (circled)*

−*make sure students have access to computers/software*

−*concerned with Johnny*
  - *great ideas, but poor production*
  - *doesn't have good computer skills*
  - *needs to be able to dictate ideas on tape or to an adult for transcription*
  - *needs to be able to use computer with word-predictive software*

Teaching/Assessment Methods

- focus on content rather than mechanics
- focus on quality rather than quantity
- begin with storyboards, guided imagery, dramatization, or projects before the writing process
- set important purposes for writing, such as writing for publication, writing to an expert, or writing to a famous person
- allow students to write in area of interest or expertise
- allow students to demonstrate understanding through alternative methods/products
- reduce or alter written requirements
- break down assignments into smaller, manageable parts
- additional time
- work with partners or small groups to confer for revising, editing, and proofreading

Assistive Technology

- voice recognition software
- organizational software
- electronic spellers and dictionaries
- tape recorder for student dictation and then transcription
- computer word processor with spelling and grammar checker or talking word processor
- portable keyboards
- word prediction software
- programs that allow writing to be read aloud
- programs that provide for audio spell checker, word prediction, and homophone distinction

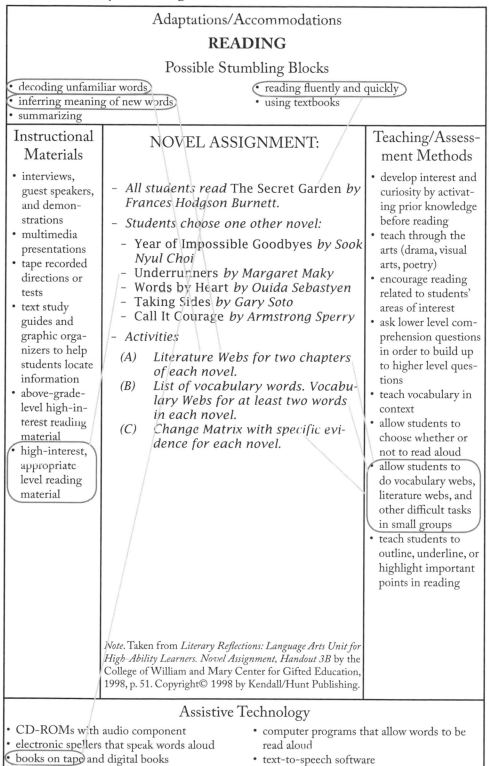

Adaptations/Accommodations
READING
Possible Stumbling Blocks

- decoding unfamiliar words
- inferring meaning of new words
- summarizing
- reading fluently and quickly
- using textbooks

Instructional Materials

- interviews, guest speakers, and demonstrations
- multimedia presentations
- tape recorded directions or tests
- text study guides and graphic organizers to help students locate information
- above-grade-level high-interest reading material
- high-interest, appropriate level reading material

NOVEL ASSIGNMENT:

- *All students read* The Secret Garden *by Frances Hodgson Burnett.*

- *Students choose one other novel:*
  - Year of Impossible Goodbyes *by Sook Nyul Choi*
  - Underrunners *by Margaret Maky*
  - Words by Heart *by Ouida Sebastyen*
  - Taking Sides *by Gary Soto*
  - Call It Courage *by Armstrong Sperry*

- *Activities*

  (A) *Literature Webs for two chapters of each novel.*

  (B) *List of vocabulary words. Vocabulary Webs for at least two words in each novel.*

  (C) *Change Matrix with specific evidence for each novel.*

Teaching/Assessment Methods

- develop interest and curiosity by activating prior knowledge before reading
- teach through the arts (drama, visual arts, poetry)
- encourage reading related to students' areas of interest
- ask lower level comprehension questions in order to build up to higher level questions
- teach vocabulary in context
- allow students to choose whether or not to read aloud
- allow students to do vocabulary webs, literature webs, and other difficult tasks in small groups
- teach students to outline, underline, or highlight important points in reading

Note. Taken from *Literary Reflections: Language Arts Unit for High-Ability Learners. Novel Assignment, Handout 3B* by the College of William and Mary Center for Gifted Education, 1998, p. 51. Copyright© 1998 by Kendall/Hunt Publishing.

Assistive Technology

- CD-ROMs with audio component
- electronic spellers that speak words aloud
- books on tape and digital books
- computer programs that allow words to be read aloud
- text-to-speech software

Adaptations/Accommodations
WRITING
Possible Stumbling Blocks

- the physical act of putting words on paper
- handwriting
- generating topics
- formulating topic sentences

- combining words into meaningful sentences
- using language mechanics effectively (e.g., grammar, punctuation, spelling)

- organizing sentences and incorporating adequate details and support statements into organized paragraphs
- revising and editing

Instructional Materials	NOTES:	Teaching/Assessment Methods
• step-by-step written directions • a proofreading checklist • scoring rubrics, models, and anchor papers for students to evaluate their own work • graphic organizers • guides such as story starters, webs, story charts, outlines • dictionaries, word banks, and thesauri • personal dictionaries of misused and misspelled words • highlighter to indicate errors/corrections • copy of teacher notes or of another student's notes (NCR paper) • pencil grips • paper with raised lines • mechanical pencils • slant board		• focus on content rather than mechanics • focus on quality rather than quantity • begin with storyboards, guided imagery, dramatization, or projects before the writing process • set important purposes for writing, such as writing for publication, writing to an expert, or writing to a famous person • allow students to write in area of interest or expertise • allow students to demonstrate understanding through alternative methods/products • reduce or alter written requirements • break down assignments into smaller, manageable parts • additional time • work with partners or small groups to confer for revising, editing, and proofreading

Assistive Technology

- voice recognition software
- organizational software
- electronic spellers and dictionaries
- tape recorder for student dictation and then transcription

- computer word processor with spelling and grammar checker or talking word processor
- portable keyboards
- word prediction software

- programs that allow writing to be read aloud
- programs that provide for audio spell checker, word prediction, and homophone distinction

Adaptations/Accommodations
READING
Possible Stumbling Blocks

- decoding unfamiliar words
- inferring meaning of new words
- summarizing
- reading fluently and quickly
- using textbooks

Instructional Materials

- interviews, guest speakers, and demonstrations
- multimedia presentations
- tape recorded directions or tests
- text study guides and graphic organizers to help students locate information
- above-grade-level high-interest reading material
- high-interest, appropriate-level reading material

NOTES:

Teaching/Assessment Methods

- develop interest and curiosity by activating prior knowledge before reading
- teach through the arts (drama, visual arts, poetry)
- encourage reading related to students' areas of interest
- ask lower level comprehension questions in order to build up to higher level questions
- teach vocabulary in context
- allow students to choose whether or not to read aloud
- allow students to do vocabulary webs, literature webs, and other difficult tasks in small groups
- teach students to outline, underline, or highlight important points in reading

Assistive Technology

- CD-ROMs with audio component
- electronic spellers that speak words aloud
- books on tape and digital books
- computer programs that allow words to be read aloud
- text-to-speech software

Adaptations/Accommodations

ORGANIZATION

Possible Stumbling Blocks

- following multistep directions
- planning the steps needed to complete a task
- organizing desk, locker, notebook, and other materials
- locating needed materials
- breaking long-range assignments into manageable steps
- prioritizing

Instructional Materials	NOTES:	Teaching/Assessment Methods
• visual models, storyboards, Venn diagrams, matrices, and flow charts • study guides that assist with locating information and answers • highlighters, index tabs, and colored stickers • assignment books and calendars for recording assignments • outlines, webs, diagrams, and other graphic organizers		• use short, simple directions • post class and homework assignments in the same area each day and assure that students record them and/or have a printed copy • verbally review class and homework assignments • work with students to establish specific due dates for short assignments and time frames for long-term assignments • break up tasks into workable and obtainable steps • provide checkpoints for long-term assignments and monitor progress frequently • provide homework hotline or structured homework assistance • provide a specific location for students to place completed work

Assistive Technology

- electronic organizers
- software organization programs
- audiotaping assignments
- e-mailing assignments from school to student's home account

Adaptations/Accommodations
MEMORY
Possible Stumbling Blocks

- concentrating and keeping track of information
- quickly recalling details
- retrieving details after time has passed

Instructional Materials	NOTES:	Teaching/Assessment Methods
• use multiple modalities when presenting directions, explanations, and instructional content • provide students with copies of the information that highlight key facts • use materials that are meaningful to students • address multiple learning styles		• have students repeat the directions or information back to teacher • have students recall important details at the end of a lesson or period of time • have students teach information to other students • deliver directions, explanations, and instructional content clearly • provide students with environmental cues and prompts such as posted rules and steps for performing tasks • provide students with written list of materials and directions • give auditory and visual cues to help students to recall information • provide adequate opportunities for repetition of information through different experiences and modalities

Assistive Technology

- teachers use software programs as an alternative or additional way of presenting information
- students tape record directions or information
- students use software programs for organization of key points

Who's Who:
Roles and Responsibilities

The list that follows gives a brief synopsis of the roles and responsibilities of the professionals who may be involved in the lives of GT/LD students.

TIPS

Teacher:
Use as a resource of roles and responsibilities in your school and school system.

Parent:
Use as a resource of the different roles and responsibilities of staff in your school and school system.

Student:
Understand the roles and identify the people in your school who can help you.

Who's Who: Roles and Responsibilities

Teacher Advisor/Case Manager (point of entry contact): Monitors students' overall progress, contacts parents regularly about progress, administers triennial reevaluations, develops IEPs, consults with classroom teachers, solves problems, and refers unresolved issues to appropriate staff.

General Education Teachers: Collaborate with special educators, instruct students in curricula, and provide accommodations and modifications.

Special Education Teachers: Ensure access to challenging and rigorous curricula, work on relevant IEP goals, accommodate and modify lessons, individually plan for and evaluate student progress, and instruct students in strategies and skills necessary to access curriculum.

Related Service Providers (Speech Language Pathologists, Occupational Therapists, Physical Therapists, etc.): Provide related services, administer evaluations, evaluate progress, develop IEPs, and support classroom teachers.

Special Education Instructional Assistants (SEIA): Support classroom instruction, provide accommodations and modifications for students, teach small group lessons, and assist teachers in any way necessary to ensure a well-run classroom environment.

Elementary and Secondary School Counselors: Schedule and counsel all students and provide information on resources; usually occurs on the middle and high school level.

Resource Teacher for Special Education (RTSE): Coordinates special education services and collaborates with and supports GT/LD coordinators, administration, educators, parents, and students.

GT/LD Instructional Specialist: Oversees GT/LD programs, helps identify and place new students, trains staff, and serves as a resource for information on GT/LD education.

Administration (Principal, Vice Principal, Student Support Specialist, etc.): Oversee schoolwide issues, monitor programs, provide instructional leadership, and serve as resources for coordinators and parents.

Consultant: An individual, independent from the school system, who provides expertise in facilitating appropriate intervention and placement decisions.

4

WHAT DO GOOD PROGRAMS AND SERVICES LOOK LIKE?

Programs and services for smart kids with learning difficulties must respond to a range of needs and abilities. These services need to be developed in all grades, and be clearly defined and articulated for parents, students, and school staff. Students need opportunities to learn at an accelerated pace, with great depth and breadth. As educators and parents, we must find a way of unleashing the potential and freeing the power within all our children regardless of gender, race, cultural background, or socioeconomic levels, to discover their interests and develop their strengths. Parents, the information here should be used as a guide to choosing and evaluating the accommodations your student receives. In addition, you may want to share this information with your child's school.

Student programming should include challenging instruction, flexible grouping, and schedules that enable students to spend time with their intellectual peers for in-depth study in all subject areas. In the elementary years, opportunities for cluster groupings of bright students need to be created within individual classrooms or grade levels, and if needed, across grade levels. Cluster groupings are groups of four to eight students at a similar instructional level. In the middle school years, gifted or advanced classes are good options for GT students with disabilities, as well as cluster grouping in all subject areas. When students reach high school, there should be opportunities for them to take honors and Advanced Placement courses in all of the major disciplines and in many of the electives offered.

There are special programs at all levels in many districts for those few students needing something very different and more intense. Opportunities might include gifted and talented elementary centers (self-contained classes of highly gifted students), gifted/LD centers (a small class in a special education setting for students identified as both gifted and disabled), magnet centers (programs with an interdisciplinary curriculum focus in particular disciplines) and International Baccalaureate programs. In 1965, the International Baccalaureate Organization (IBO) established a program of studies to ensure high-quality educational standards for students studying in international schools throughout the world. The IBO offers an internationally recognized diploma based on in-depth study of major content areas.

Students should be encouraged to try the advanced courses and programs at all levels if they demonstrate the motivation for advanced studies and/or have the prerequisites needed. Students with learning challenges may need the supports of special education providers, counselors, and other specialists to be successful in the more rigorous and challenging classes. For some students, the appropriate accommodations and adaptations will be the key to their success. Under no circumstances should students with unique needs and strengths be excluded from these opportunities.

> For some students, the appropriate accommodations and adaptations will be the key to their success.

Options for the Education of Bright Students With Learning Difficulties

Many public school systems and private schools have put in place a consultative program to meet the needs of bright students with learning challenges. A specialist with expertise in the education of these students helps the other school staff, particularly the classroom teachers, to utilize the best practices in providing appropriate education.

Schools and school systems without identified specialists should designate someone to perform this role. Typically a GT teacher, special educator, counselor, or administrator will take on leadership in this area. The following task analysis illustrates the process that these specialists undertake as they create rigorous and supportive programs for their bright underachieving students:

- Analyze what the roles and responsibilities of the educators are within the school.
- Assign the roles and responsibilities to the educators within the school.
- Set a collaborative climate. Team planning facilitates inclusion of these students in the regular classroom.
- Collect and study data related to the students (e.g., test scores, performance in school, performance in the community).
- Extend each child's intellectual boundaries and help all students achieve their highest potential.
- Identify all students who have the capability, motivation, or potential to accept the challenge of taking honors, AP, and advanced-level courses, and provide them with the opportunity to do so.
- Focus on students' strengths and interests. Ensure that differentiated educational programs and/or services are systematically provided for bright students in all grades, including students with learning disabilities or other special needs.

- Provide accelerated and enriched instruction, including appropriate strategy and skill instruction and instructional adaptations and accommodations while implementing students' IEPs, 504 Plans, or other less formal plans.
- Analyze curricula to identify key concepts.
- Collect resources and materials (e.g., curricular guides, programs, software).
- Choose appropriate resources, materials, strategies, and techniques.
- Plan for alternative learning activities.
- Plan units and lessons.
- Collect appropriate adaptations and accommodations for each student.
- Implement units and lessons.
- Plan for assessments that capitalize on students' strengths and work around the weaknesses.
- Evaluate successful/best practices.
- Schedule team meetings to discuss students. Specific weekly, bimonthly, or monthly meeting times allow for ongoing planning and an opportunity to discuss and evaluate student progress. Difficulties are addressed before they multiply and escalate.
- Know and understand the social/emotional profile of each student in order to provide strategies that alleviate frustration and create motivation and interest in school learning.
- Train teachers (possibly during in-service) on working with smart students with learning challenges, including their characteristics, needs, strategies, adaptations, and accommodations.
- Train students and parents on various resources, materials, and strategies.
- Keep lines of communication open between and among staff, students, and parents.

Self-Contained Public School Programs

Three public school programs have had ongoing, comprehensive programs for meeting the needs of twice-exceptional students. These programs are located in Montgomery

County, MD; in Westchester, NY; and in Albuquerque, NM. The Montgomery County Public Schools GT/LD program is described in detail below, both as an example of best practices in action and as a guide for parents or school systems that may be interested in developing a similar program (Weinfeld et al., 2002).

The Montgomery County Public Schools Program

Determined to address the needs of their gifted and learning disabled students, educators in MCPS have spent many years creating a dynamic, comprehensive program for their gifted and learning-disabled student population. In 1986, MCPS initiated a pilot program to explore the incidence rate of students with high cognitive ability that were experiencing learning difficulties (Starnes, Ginevan, Stokes, & Barton, 1988). With initial funding from the Jacob K. Javits Gifted and Talented Education Grant, promising developments have occurred in the Montgomery County Public Schools. MCPS identifies gifted students with varying degrees of learning disabilities and has developed special self-contained classes for gifted students with severe learning disabilities while those with moderate and mild disabilities receive services in general education classes (Starnes et al.).

GT/LD students in grades 2–12 receive appropriate instruction, adaptations, and accommodations related to their disability. Successful, practical programming is based on solid research and theory. GT/LD students are guaranteed access to accelerated and enriched instruction that maintains the rigor and high standards expected of all gifted students. As with other gifted students, the range of instructional opportunities available to GT/LD students are provided in gifted classes in elementary and middle school, in honors and Advanced Placement classes at the high school, in highly selective gifted and magnet programs in grades 4–12, and through differentiation in general education classes at all levels. In addition, GT/LD students with severe learning disabilities receive appropriate gifted instruction within GT/LD Center Programs. Gifted underachieving students also have the opportunity to participate in a mentor program designed to nurture talents and develop potential. The comprehensiveness of the delivery of GT/LD programming is what makes this one of the unique programs serving this population.

The MCPS model is also unique because it simultaneously addresses the giftedness and the academic needs of each student regardless of his or her grade level or the severity of his or her disability. Overseeing all of the instructional and program opportunities is a full-time program coordinator with expertise in both gifted education and special education. Drawing on the best practices others have researched, and from its teachers' and administrators' own field experiences, MCPS has combined the most successful components of teaching GT/LD students into a strength-based, integrated, and collaborative program.

The following profile is a snapshot of a student-centered classroom with a view into the workings, resources, and climate for students within the MCPS GT/LD Center Programs:

> The room was a buzz of activity. Steven was working on an independent study project at a computer as he listened to a book that had been converted from text to speech. A group of students was sitting and working at a round table with a variety of resource materials related to their in-depth study of whales. Rachel, returning from her social studies mainstream class, began dictating a biographical sketch on Sacagawea into a tape recorder. Frank was meeting with the teacher at the front table about the next steps in his research project. Student products from their Structures unit lined the bookcases under the windows. The student-made three-dimensional projects reflected concepts learned in both math and science. Junior Great Books, software products, reference materials, large-print books, science equipment, and math equipment filled the shelves. On the walls of the classroom, colorful posters, class standards and expectations, message boards, and plans for the day were displayed. The workstations had a collection of tools that were always available to the students—pens, pencils, tape recorders, graphic organizers, NCR paper (carbonless copy paper), electronic spellers, and calculators.

Note that in this classroom, the activity is purposeful and planned, and the interdisciplinary instruction and multiple tools and opportunities for choice are the norm.

The first MCPS Center Program for gifted and learning-disabled students opened in 1987 for fourth and fifth graders. Since that time, this program has expanded across the county to its present level of three primary (grades 2–3) and three upper level (grades 4–5) programs housed in three separate elementary schools, as well as three middle school programs and three high school programs. The instructional program has focused on developing strengths; providing classroom organization that is flexible and collaborative to maximize goal setting, self-direction, group discussion, self-reflection, problem solving, and self-evaluation; and providing curriculum and instruction that is inquiry-based with a thinking focus.

While the vast majority of gifted students with learning disabilities in MCPS are served in their home schools with varying degrees of support and accommodations, GT/LD students who are not demonstrating academic progress in their home schools are considered for the GT/LD Center Programs. The GT/LD Center Programs serve students who have both a documented superior cognitive ability and an identified learning disability. The majority of students accepted into the program score two standard deviations above the mean (130) on at least one of the four indices of the WISC-IV, or comparable intelligence scales. Identification of the gift does not rely solely on broad IQ scores. Strong performance on IQ subtests, as well as other less formal evidence of giftedness is considered. Strengths of these students often include superior ability in forming concepts, abstract reasoning, vocabulary, creativity, math reasoning, science, and the arts.

In addition to superior cognitive ability, GT/LD students demonstrate a significant learning disability with academic deficits that are severe enough to drive the need for reduced staff-student ratio and special education supports throughout the day. Learning-disabled students, as defined by state regulations, have a deficit in one or more of the basic psychological processes involved in understanding or using language. The deficit affects performance in one or more of the areas of written language, reading, or mathematics. The GT/LD Center Programs serve students who demonstrate academic deficits that are severe, so that barriers to achievement cannot be overcome through accommodations and modifications in the student's home school. These Center Programs provide access to GT instruction for students who would not have access otherwise.

An Individualized Education Plan (IEP) team considers this placement as part of the school-based periodic or annual IEP review meeting. The school IEP teams refer students who are candidates for this program to their local supervisor of special education. A small committee of individuals who are familiar with the GT/LD program and the characteristics of the students in the program then conduct a review of the candidate. The committee includes the program coordinator for GT/LD programs, a representative from the GT department, and a school psychologist. If a difference of opinion regarding the placement exists, or if there is a need to clarify certain issues, the case is considered by the central IEP team, which then identifies the appropriate placement. The goal is to serve students in their home school, therefore, students placed in the GT/LD Center Program must demonstrate a limited response to their home school's attempt to modify the student's program and provide sufficient interventions over a significant period of time.

At all grade levels in Montgomery County, students in GT/LD Center Programs receive instruction that focuses on developing their strengths and improving existing skills in their areas of weakness. The GT/LD programs are housed in general education school facilities, enabling students to participate with their nondisabled peers wherever possible. Students may enter and exit the program at any grade level. Students typically are mainstreamed for physical education and the arts, as well as lunch and other general activities. They are later mainstreamed in other subject areas as they demonstrate readiness to handle the academic and organizational demands of those subjects. Students typically need special education staff in the classroom with them as they begin their mainstream experiences. As students near the point of exiting the program, they have developed the self-advocacy and compensatory skills necessary to handle the mainstream environment without direct staff support. Middle school and high school students are generally ready for participation in the mainstream. General educators at the secondary level also tend to be specialists in their content areas and, whenever possible, it is beneficial for students to have access to these specialists.

Therefore, the middle school and high school models incorporate more team-teaching situations, giving GT/LD students opportunities to participate in the mainstream with additional support. Similarly, both as a result of having spent several years in the program and because of their developmental maturity, more of the middle and high school students are able to take responsibility for their own accommodations and learning. More students are ready to exit the program at the upper grades than lower grade levels. The elementary GT/LD programs have a greater focus on the teaching and development of skills and compensatory strategies, while the secondary programs have more of a focus on implementing these skills and strategies throughout content areas. At every grade level, the primary focus remains on developing the gifts of these students.

The GT/LD classes are staffed in the same way as other special education programs for students with severe learning disabilities. The teachers are all special education certified and receive ongoing training in the education of gifted and talented students. A full-time program coordinator helps manage all of these programs, and provides consultation and training for all staff working with GT/LD students.

Implementation of effective instructional programming for GT/LD students has been a collaborative effort between the district's Division of Accelerated and Enriched Instruction (Gifted and Talented Office) and its Department of Special Education during the last 15 years. This collaboration has provided an opportunity to draw on what is known to be the best practices from both special education and gifted education (Brody & Mills, 1997). The ongoing dialogue and trust between the departments has built a partnership that serves students well.

Each of the three regionally located elementary schools serves as a home to two special GT/LD classrooms. Students typically spend a majority of their academic day in these special classrooms, which are staffed with one special education teacher and one paraeducator. Class sizes vary, but on average there are 8–12 students. The focus of the elementary program is to provide students with instruction in their areas of strength while simultaneously working to improve areas affected by their disabilities. Students become familiar with accommodations, such as computer software programs, that can work around their disabilities. A multisensory approach allows students to utilize and recognize their areas of strength. As students demonstrate proficiency in various subject areas and progress to the point that they can be successful, they may be mainstreamed for part of the day, with appropriate support and accommodations. When mainstreamed, students are included with their nondisabled peers in classes that provide the appropriate rigor and challenge they need.

Each of the three regionally located middle schools serves as a home to students who are GT/LD and who need special education support for a majority of their academic day. Students may be placed in a special education classroom for instruction in their areas of disability. They are typically placed in small classes with other GT/LD students in English and reading, but they are usually placed in the mainstream classroom with their nondisabled gifted peers for social studies and science. A special educator often provides direct support in these classes, sometimes through a team-teaching approach. Depending on the strengths and needs of an individual student, math may be delivered in a self-contained, special education class, a supported mainstream class, or a fully mainstreamed setting. An additional period for providing special education instruction may be offered through the secondary resource room. The resource room may provide instruction in areas addressed in an individual student's IEP, such as learning skills, thinking skills, communication skills, technology skills, and interpersonal skills. Case managers in these GT/LD settings have a smaller than typical staff to student ratio, allowing for more intensive communication with other school staff, as well as with parents. Case managers work with students to help them to understand their unique strengths and needs and to help them to increasingly be able to advocate on their own for accommodations that will allow them access to accelerated and enriched instruction. Students typically spend more and more of their time in mainstream classes during the course of their middle school years.

Most students who have participated in the elementary and/or middle school special GT/LD settings are ready to enter their home high schools or highly gifted magnet programs. There they may receive the support of a secondary resource period(s) and a case manager as they take on the challenge of high school offerings, including honors and/or Advanced Placement courses. Students who need the more intensive support of a special GT/LD setting may be served at one of the three regionally located high schools that house the Secondary Learning Center Program. In addition to the secondary resource period(s), students may receive special education instruction alongside Learning Center students, in a variety of academic course offerings. The Learning Center classes offer a special classroom setting, with a reduced student to staff ratio. There are typically not enough students who are GT/LD to comprise an entire class, so the instruction for students who are GT/LD in these classes must be differentiated for their cognitive level.

However, most students who are identified as GT/LD typically are in mainstream classes for the vast majority of their day. Case managers in these settings have a smaller than typical staff to student ratio, allowing for more intensive communication with staff, parents, and students. There is a special education assistive technology center in each of the schools, staffed by a paraeducator throughout the day. Students or their teachers may arrange for students to receive extra accommodations, including the use of word processors, text-to-speech software, speech-to-text software, or special education assistance in this special center at any time during the school day.

In each of the high school programs, one special class is identified in each of the four academic areas—English, social studies, science, and math—at each grade level. One designated teacher has one period of his or her day designated as a magnet class, which includes GT/LD and underachieving GT students, along with typical GT students. The teacher chosen to lead this class has shown exemplary skills in utilizing adaptations and accommodations and in nurturing students in the past. He or she agrees to participate in three day-long trainings on effective practices for use with GT/LD students. This pilot program began at the ninth grade level in the 2004–05 school year and will be phasing up one grade level each year. If results warrant success, this model could be extended to all high schools. More information on this pilot program and MCPS' GT/LD programs can be found at http://www.mcps.k12.md.us.

Talent Development

Bright students, especially those with learning challenges, must be provided opportunities that focus on their gifts, enabling them not only to develop a positive self-concept, but also the realization of their potential. Project High Hopes, the Schoolwide Enrichment Model (Renzulli & Reis, 1997), and the Wings Mentor Program, are examples of successful programs that have been developed on this principle.

Project High Hopes, developed by Susan Baum, Carolyn R. Cooper, Terry W. Neu, and Steve Owen (1997), has a curriculum designed to help middle school teachers develop student talents. Student talents are identified and, through authentic problem-solving experiences, the students gain a deep understanding of the principles of science and technology and the visual and performing arts.

The Schoolwide Enrichment Model, developed by Joseph S. Renzulli, consists of activities for individuals and small groups to investigate real-world problems by using appropriate methods of inquiry. Teachers are responsible for helping students focus an area of concern into a solvable problem. The next step is to provide them with the tools necessary to solve the problem and assist them in communicating their results to an authentic audience.

Beginning in 1989, the Wings Mentor Program in Maryland's Montgomery County Public Schools was developed to provide additional support to GT/LD students who were not succeeding in the classroom (Shevitz, Weinfeld, Jeweler & Barnes-Robinson, 2003). The goal of this program was to provide students with the opportunity for a successful learning experience by pairing them with mentors who would nurture them, while increasing their knowledge and skills in an area of interest. The program was designed to focus on the students' strengths and their potential for success, in order to enhance their self-esteem and self-confidence. The intent of the program was to provide students with the stimulation and motivation needed to enable them to begin to be successful in school. The Wings Mentor Program was founded on four basic principles:

- *Focus on strength.* The focus for gifted underachieving students is on their abilities. In the mentor program, the attention is directed to the students' strengths and interests, and their potential for success.
- *Build success.* The program is designed to maximize student success. By working one-on-one with a mentor in an area of interest, the program provides the students with an opportunity to be successful and gain an awareness of their abilities.
- *Enhance self-esteem.* Through their successes, students gain self-confidence, which in turn may contribute to increased self-esteem. A desired outcome is that the students will become excited about school and begin to believe in themselves.
- *Plant a seed.* The intent of the program is to plant seeds for future success. Although the program may not be able to reverse the patterns of underachievement in such a limited time, it may serve as a catalyst for positive change.

Obtaining the right mentors is crucial to the effectiveness of the program. In the Wings program, the mentors have a strong education background or have experience working with children. They are carefully screened and selected based on their knowledge and their ability to share their skills with young people. Although newly acquired knowledge and the final products the students create are important, the relationship that develops between the mentor and the student is most significant. During weekly meetings, the mentor guides the students in an area of study and provides them with needed support. Although they are not counselors, they are trained to be constantly aware of and sensitive to the student's self-concept and to weave self-esteem building strategies into their work where appropriate. It is the mentor to student relationship that is a catalyst for improving the students' view of themselves, empowering them to be successful in the classroom.

The mentors meet with their students during the school day for an hour each week for 8 weeks. During these sessions students explore their selected topics of interest. Some students take this unique time to study in-depth an existing area of passion, while others use the time to explore new areas. The students direct their own learning, while acquiring skills in problem solving, planning, goal setting, research, and organization. Most importantly, the mentors help the students learn new strategies and methods to circumvent their weaknesses, allowing them to demonstrate what they have learned in their areas of strength. Over the course of the mentor sessions, students develop and complete a final project that reflects what they have learned. The products are typically hands-on and experiential, enabling the students to gain awareness of their capabilities and learning styles.

> *It is the mentor to student relationship that is a catalyst for improving the students' view of themselves, empowering them to be successful in the classroom.*

Students present their projects to an appropriate audience, usually in their classroom. The final product and presentation are an integral aspect of the program because it provides a means of holding the students accountable for their time with the mentor and creates a way for the students to share their knowledge and experience with classmates. When the students make their presentations, their peers and teachers often recognize their gifts and talents for the first time. In many cases, the success of the project helps to change the student's self-perception. By accentuating the strengths and minimizing the student's areas of weakness, the mentor program increases the student's self-concept and self-esteem. It is a powerful tool for changing peer and teacher perceptions, as well as self-perceptions.

Marking the culmination of the program is Show-off Night, a special evening when the students come to display their projects, share their experiences, and celebrate their accomplishments. While the argument can be made that every student could benefit from the unique one-on-one attention that a mentor has to offer, the program is critical to those who are at risk of failing and, yet, possess such great potential.

Private School Options

Many private or independent schools do an excellent job of providing appropriate education for bright students with learning challenges. Some of these schools have certified special education staff, and are accredited by their states to implement students' Individual Educational Plans. Other schools may not be state approved as special education schools, but still may do an outstanding job of providing the challenge, supports, and specialized instruction GT/LD students need.

When evaluating whether any private school may be a good fit for your child, parents, you should scrutinize the program in the same way you would a public school program. First, you will want to see the ways the school provides challenging instruction that will help your child to fulfill his or her potential. Secondly, you will need to look for evidence that teachers routinely employ a variety of adaptations and accommodations so that all students can access rigorous instruction. You will want to examine the strategies and interventions the schools use to help students improve their weaker academic areas, as well as their behavioral and attention skills, including self-advocacy skills. Finally, you will want to look for evidence of effective case management that brings you and the school staff together into a partnership for the benefit of the individual students.

TIPS and Tools: Supplementary Materials

Included in this section:

- The Animal School: Bright Animals With Learning Difficulties
- Task Analysis Checklist for Programs and Services
- What to Look for in a School Checklist
- Program and Service Options Checklist
- Student and Parent Interviews

The Animal School: Bright Animals With Learning Difficulties

George Reavis wrote *The Animal School: A Fable* when he was the Assistant Superintendent of the Cincinnati Public Schools in the 1940s. Rich Weinfeld has adapted Reavis's fable to apply to smart kids with learning challenges. They each have a great educational message.

TIPS

Teacher:
Read the fable to the class. Discuss the meaning. Give to parents at conference time. Use in training sessions.

Parent:
Read the fable. Share with teachers and discuss the meaning. Share with your child. Discuss the meaning with your child and how it applies to issues he or she may be facing.

Student:
Read the fable. Think about how it relates to you, a friend, or a person in your classroom or in your community activities.

The Animal School: Bright Animals With Learning Difficulties

Once upon a time, the animals decided they must do something to prepare their young to face the challenges of the world, and so they organized a school. They adopted an activity curriculum consisting of running, climbing, swimming, and flying, and to make sure all animals were competent in all of the important skills, all the animals had to take all of the subjects.

The Duck was an excellent swimmer, better in fact than his instructor, and made passing grades in flying, but he was very poor in running. Because he was slow in running, he had to stay after school and also spend less time swimming, in order to spend more time practicing his running. This was continued until his webbed feet were badly worn and he was only average in swimming. But, average was acceptable in the new animal school, so nobody worried about that except the Duck.

The Rabbit started at the top of his class in running, but he had a nervous breakdown because of so much make-up work in swimming.

The Squirrel was excellent in climbing until he developed frustration in the flying class, where his teacher made him start from the ground up instead of from the treetop down. His feelings of frustration spilled over to his other classes and he ended up with a C in climbing and a D in running.

The newest student in the school was an abnormal animal called the Snakehead Fish. At the end of the year the snakehead, which could swim very well and also climb out of the water and walk on the land, was the valedictorian of the school.

Task Analysis Checklist for Programs and Services

The following task analysis illustrates the process that specialists undertake as they create rigorous and supportive programs for their bright underachieving students.

TIPS

Teacher:
Use as a self-evaluation checklist. Use when you're planning accommodations for students. Use as a communication tool with parents, other staff members, and students.

Parent:
Use as an evaluation tool of your child's school experience. Use it for creating questions to ask at conferences and other meetings.

Student:
Look at the Task Analysis checklist to see if you want to add any information that would be important for your parents and teachers to know.

Task Analysis Checklist for Programs and Services

_____ Analyze what the roles and responsibilities of the educators are within the school.

_____ Assign the roles and responsibilities to the educators within the school.

_____ Set a collaborative climate. Team planning facilitates inclusion of these students in the regular classroom.

_____ Collect and study data related to the students (e.g., test scores, performance in school, and performance in the community).

_____ Extend each child's intellectual boundaries and help all students achieve their highest potential.

_____ Identify and provide for students who have the capability, motivation, or potential to accept the challenges of honors, AP, and advanced-level courses the opportunity to do so.

_____ Focus on students' strengths and interests. Ensure that differentiated educational programs and/or services are systematically provided for bright students in all grades, including students with learning disabilities or other special needs.

_____ Provide accelerated and enriched instruction, including appropriate strategy and skill instruction, instructional adaptations, and accommodations, while implementing students' IEPs and/or 504 Plans.

_____ Analyze curricula to identify key concepts.

_____ Collect resources and materials (e.g., curricula guides, programs, software).

_____ Choose appropriate resources, materials, strategies, and techniques.

_____ Plan for alternative learning activities.

_____ Plan units and lessons.

_____ Collect appropriate adaptations and accommodations for each student.

_____ Implement units and lessons.

_____ Plan for assessments that capitalize on students' strengths and obviate weaknesses.

_____ Evaluate successful/best practices.

Task Analysis Checklist for Programs and Services, continued

_____ Schedule team meetings to discuss students. Specific weekly, bimonthly, or monthly meeting times allow for ongoing planning and an opportunity to discuss and evaluate student progress. This way, difficulties are addressed before they multiply and escalate.

_____ Know and understand the social/emotional profile of each student in order to provide strategies that alleviate frustration and create motivation and interest in school learning.

_____ Train teachers on aspects of smart students with learning challenges, including their characteristics, needs, strategies, adaptations, and accommodations.

_____ Train students and parents on available resources, materials, and strategies.

_____ Keep lines of communication open between and among staff, students, and parents.

What to Look For in a School Checklist

A school is a vibrant community of learners. The following checklist includes specifics that help define a good school environment.

TIPS

Teacher:
Use the checklist as a positive evaluation tool for your school and classroom.

Parent:
Use the checklist as a positive evaluation tool. Talk to educators and other parents at your school about what makes a good school. Become involved as a volunteer. Keep a positive perspective.

What to Look for in a School Checklist

School Data

- Vision or mission statement _____
- Staff and staff supports _____
- Curriculum _____
- Level of academic rigor _____
- Extracurricular offerings _____
- Grading and reporting policy _____
- Test scores _____

Climate

- Positive tone _____
- Respect _____
- Comfort _____
- Supportive environment _____
- Students engaged in purposeful activities _____
- Challenging environment _____
- Interactive environment _____
- Risk-taking environment _____
- Flexible environment _____
- Visible standards and expectations _____
- Technologically up-to-date _____
- Open communication among educators, parents, and students _____

Organization

- Grouping _____
- Team teaching _____
- Flexible schedules _____

Programs

- Challenging instruction _____
- Flexible grouping and schedules _____
- Strength-based instruction _____
- Differentiated instruction _____

Management

- Consistent behavior expectations _____
- High academic expectations _____
- Collaborative _____
- Positive reinforcement _____
- Sense of humor _____
- Timely feedback _____
- Efficient record keeping _____
- Evaluation _____

Self-Advocacy Opportunities _____

Attention to Social/Emotional Principles _____

Variety of Materials, Resources, and Activities _____

Program and Service Options Checklist

The following checklist should aid you in evaluating the GT/LD program in your school and other outside programs.

TIPS

Teacher:
Use information to provide contacts and resources.

Parent:
Use to guide decision making about programs for your child. Use to provide your school system with information about exemplary programs.

Student:
Use information to find out how kids like you are being challenged and supported in other places.

Program and Service Options Checklist

The following services and/or programs are examples of those that may be available in schools:

Local Public Schools
(Sources: school system Web site, school principal, school counselor, GT specialist)

The school in consideration offers:

_____ Talent development programs
_____ GT/LD services
_____ GT services
_____ LD services

Evidence of:

_____ instruction in the student's area of strength
_____ opportunities for the instruction of skills and strategies in academic areas that are affected by the student's challenges
_____ an appropriately differentiated program, including individualized instructional adaptations and accommodations systematically provided to students
_____ comprehensive case management to coordinate all aspects of the student's Individual Educational Plan
_____ rigorous instruction
_____ clear roles and responsibilities
_____ attention to social/emotional issues

Other Public Schools
(Sources: state department of education Web site, state GT coordinator, special education coordinator, private advocates)

Does the school in consideration offer:

_____ Talent development programs
_____ GT/LD services
_____ GT services
_____ LD services

Evidence of:

_____ instruction in the student's area of strength
_____ opportunities for the instruction of skills and strategies in academic areas that are affected by the student's challenges
_____ an appropriately differentiated program, including individualized instructional adaptations and accommodations systematically provided to students

Program and Service Options Checklist, continued

_____ comprehensive case management to coordinate all aspects of the student's Individual Educational Plan
_____ rigorous instruction
_____ clear roles and responsibilities
_____ attention to social/emotional issues

Private Sector
(Sources: private school Web sites, local colleges and universities, private advocates)

Does the school/program in consideration offer:
_____ Talent development programs
_____ GT/LD services
_____ GT services
_____ LD services

Evidence of:
_____ instruction in the student's area of strength
_____ opportunities for the instruction of skills and strategies in academic areas that are affected by the student's challenges
_____ an appropriately differentiated program, including individualized instructional adaptations and accommodations systematically provided to students
_____ comprehensive case management to coordinate all aspects of the student's Individual Educational Plan
_____ rigorous instruction
_____ clear roles and responsibilities
_____ attention to social/emotional issues

Student and Parent Interviews

When the focus of learning is on a student's strengths and interests, rather than on his or her areas of weakness, then self-confidence and self-esteem are increased and he or she is more likely to be successful. Interviews are one way to obtain information on student strengths and interests.

TIPS

Teacher:
Use the Student Interview questions to help you identify your student's strengths and interests. Use the Parent Interview questions to gain information about the student. When planning instruction for the student, work through these strengths whenever possible. The questions are also helpful when trying to match your student with a mentor.

Parent:
Ask yourself the parent questions when trying to identify your child's strengths and interests. Share the information with the teacher.

Student:
Ask yourself the student questions to help you identify your strengths and interests.

Parent Interview

1. What does your child choose to do in his or her free time?

2. What are your child's interests in school?

3. What are your child's interests outside of school?

4. What are your child's hobbies?

5. On what type of school projects is your child most successful?

6. What do you see as your child's strengths, abilities, or expertise?

7. What does your child like to talk about?

8. What does your child read about?

9. How does your child choose to show what he or she knows?

Student Interview

1. What do you choose to do in your free time?

2. What are your interests in school?

3. What are your interests outside of school?

4. What are your hobbies?

5. On what type of school projects are you most successful?

6. What do you see as your strengths, abilities, or areas of expertise?

7. What do you like to talk about?

8. What do you read about?

9. How do you choose to show what you know?

Student Interview, continued

10. If you could study anything that you wanted, what would you choose to study?

11. How did you become interested in this topic?

12. What have you done on your own (outside of school) in this area?

13. Would you like to work with a mentor (someone who helps you work on projects that interest you)? What is it about working with a mentor that appeals to you?

14. If you could study the topic from Question 10 with a mentor, what types of things are you interested in having a mentor do with you on this topic?

15. How do you like to learn? (For example, do you learn best through books, movies, museums, hands-on experiences, interviewing people, or other methods?)

16. What type of product do you like to develop best? (For example, do you prefer to do an essay, a poster, a movie, a PowerPoint™ presentation, a model, a speech, or another type of product?)

5

WHAT ACTIONS ENSURE THAT OUR SMART KIDS WILL OVERCOME THEIR LEARNING DISABILITIES?

Mr. and Mrs. Anderson were relieved and somewhat surprised as they left the team meeting for their son, Matthew, at his new school. Matthew was a complicated student with great gifts and significant challenges. In the past, they had received many contacts from the school about the problems that existed, but few positive comments or solutions. This year they had been called to come to the school before the year even began to plan for Matthew's first year in middle school.

Matthew's English teacher, who was also the sixth-grade team leader, volunteered to tell all of the staff about the appropriate adaptations and accommodations Matthew would need. The teacher described the special education instruction that she would be providing to address Matthew's needs in writing and organization. The team leader would coordinate the communication between the general educators, Matthew, and his parents, as well as communicate regularly with the special education teacher. The team leader spoke about how bright Matthew was and that he should be involved in some GT classes.

The special educator said she would communicate with the counselor, who suggested that Matthew participate in a new group to help students advocate for themselves when talking with teachers about their strengths and needs. Matthew agreed to participate in the counseling group and to check in with the resource teacher at the beginning and end of each day to clarify his assignments and make sure he had the needed materials. Mr. and Mrs. Anderson agreed to check Matthew's planbook each night and communicate to staff via e-mail on a regular basis.

The team recommended that Matthew start the year in GT classes for science and social studies with a review before the second marking period began to evaluate his progress and to make recommendations for the next marking period. The principal reviewed each person's responsibilities and set the date for a progress review. Mr. and Mrs. Anderson and Matthew left the meeting feeling optimistic that the new school year would be Matthew's best yet.

Matthew's success that school year was aided by a team approach implemented by the educators who serve gifted students with learning disabilities in his home school.

Making It Happen

Designing a dynamic classroom where students are successful does not happen serendipitously. It requires careful analysis, planning, and thoughtful implementation. Key to its success is the educator's adoption of the underlying belief that these students are gifted first and their learning challenges come second. Once this is firmly embedded in one's attitude, developing a climate in which the students feel safe and can achieve success is a natural outcome. Providing appropriate accommodations with the understanding that one is leveling the playing field rather than giving unfair advantage is also key to a student's success (Weinfeld et al., 2002).

General education teachers are expected to teach students who exhibit a wide range of needs. They often fail to identify twice-exceptional students, however, because these students may be able to compensate for their disabilities with their giftedness. It is essential that the general education teacher know that gifts and disabilities often mask each other, and that these students are likely to exhibit variable performance and social/emotional difficulties (Landrum, 1989). These students may appear to possess average abilities, but are really performing well below their potential (Baum, 1990; Brody & Mills, 1997).

It is important for educators to keep in mind that the writing, organization, memory, and reading skills of these students are likely to impact their success across all subject areas. In planning, it is crucial that the teacher consider instructional methods and strategies that either circumvent the student's difficulties or that build in the necessary scaffolding to empower students to be successful with the demands of the assignment.

Educators can build in the necessary scaffolding by analyzing the obstacles that would prevent a student from accessing rigorous instruction. Once the student's obstacles have been identified, educators should reference the menu of possible interventions and choose those that will provide access to appropriate enriched and accelerated instruction (for more information, see Bordering on Excellence materials at the end of Chapter 3).

Training

The success of any program is dependent upon the training of those who work with twice-exceptional students. Training should focus on the definition, identification, and best practices to use in programming for these students. Some universities offer undergraduate and graduate courses specific to identification and appropriate services for bright students with learning disabilities. County, state, and national conferences or institutes on topics related to the instruction of these students also provide good training grounds for staff. Professional leave is often granted so educators may participate in these sessions, with the intent of learning the material and implementing it with their students. Training is also accomplished during school-based in-service workshops, staff meetings, and team or individual meetings.

During school-based, half-day or full-day training sessions, schools can address a variety of topics related to these students. The administrator, special education staff, counselor, GT staff, and grade-level teams should collaborate on meeting the needs of these students within the school. Based on a student's needs assessment, in-service workshops are designed to introduce and/or develop instructional resources, materials, and strategies to be used with students. For example, in-service workshops may include topics such as building positive attitudes; a deeper understanding of the characteristics, strengths, and needs of this population; conflict resolution strategies; strategies for integrating arts instruction into content areas; thinking strategies such as Bloom's Taxonomy and Edward de Bono's (1986) Thinking Hats; utilizing mentors; and strategies on how to differentiate instruction. Training also should include a review of current successful practices in the areas of reading, writing, organization, memory, metacognition, and the use of technology.

Staff meetings are a good time for training. Due to the shorter length of this type of meeting, one concept, strategy, idea, or issue is addressed. For example, keeping up-to-date on current research is important, so in this type of forum, a recent journal article related to GT/LD students may be distributed and discussed with staff members.

Team or individual meetings offer excellent opportunities for training. The resource teacher shares with a teacher or team an effective adaptation or accommodation for these students. In this setting, questions, concerns, and plans are focused on individual students and their individual strengths and needs.

The immediate transfer and application of this type of training takes place in the classroom.

Develop and Initiate Action Plans

The following plans of action are designed for educators, parents, and students. There are four consistent components: training, collaborative formulation of educational plans, ongoing communication, and evaluation. Each of these is crucial if effective adaptations and accommodations are to be provided to bright students with learning challenges.

Action Plan for Educators

1. Special educators and general educators should complete training on:

   - the definition, identification, and best practices in programming for twice-exceptional students and bright underachieving students;
   - understanding the assessment data that relates to these students;
   - understanding appropriate resources, materials, strategies, and techniques to be used both in instruction and assessments that allow students to demonstrate their skills without the interference of their disabilities;
   - understanding how to capitalize on students' strengths; and
   - the need to evaluate and revise adaptations and accommodations.

2. Include general educators as part of the IEP, 504 Plan, or child study team while formulating adaptations and accommodations.

3. Schedule ongoing face-to-face meetings between special educators and general educators to plan for implementation of the student's IEP or 504 Plan, and child study plan, including needed adaptations and accommodations. Meetings should include a discussion of the

reason for each adaptation and accommodation as it relates to the individual student's disability.

4. Build in an evaluation component to look at the efficacy of each adaptation and accommodation with a plan of fading them out over time, allowing students to move from dependence to independence.

Action Plan for Parents

1. Parents should participate in training on:

   - the definition, identification, and best practices in programming for their children;
   - the possible negative effects of providing excessive or unnecessary accommodations;
   - the need to select accommodations based on the impact of the individual student's disability or learning challenges;
   - the need to move students from dependence to independence; and
   - the need to evaluate and revise adaptations and accommodations.

2. Parents should take part in the IEP, 504 Plan, or child study team while it is formulating adaptations and accommodations.

3. Ongoing face-to-face meetings between school staff members and parents should occur to monitor implementation of the student's plan, including needed adaptations and accommodations.

4. Build in an evaluation component to look at the efficacy of each adaptation and accommodation with a plan of fading them out over time, allowing students to move from dependence to independence.

Action Plan for Students

1. Students should participate in training that stresses:

   - understanding their own unique strengths and weaknesses;
   - understanding how specific adaptations and accom-

modations maximize their strengths, while minimizing their weaknesses;

- understanding and implementing advocacy and communication strategies; and
- understanding the need to move from dependence to independence.

2. Include students as part of the IEP, 504 Plan, or child study team, in the formulation of adaptations and ac-commodations.
3. Schedule ongoing face-to-face meetings between school staff and students to monitor implementation of the student's plan, including needed adaptations and accommodations.
4. Ensure student participation in a periodic evaluation component to look at the efficacy of each adaptation and accommodation with a plan of fading them out over time, allowing students to move from dependence to independence.

From LD to Ph.D.: Postsecondary Education

What happens to smart kids with learning difficulties when they leave high school? Most of them go to colleges and universities and grow into productive, creative young professionals. Their choice in schools is as diverse as they are, from 2- and 4-year institutions, to art and trade institutes, to Ivy League universities. Their stories are inspiring and their accomplishments are extraordinary. They have stories of unleashed potential and real-ized dreams, where it is OK to imagine a world without barriers, and to set seemingly unattainable goals. These are talented young people who have overcome the barriers and frustrations that come with having learning difficulties or attention problems.

All students face the challenge of finding the right place to continue with their postsecondary education. Parents and kids need to know that there are wonderful schools to meet a variety of student needs, as well as the support to help find the right one for your child. Libraries and bookstores have reference guides to colleges and universities for students with learning and attention difficulties. There are professionals who specialize in working with students and families during the process of selecting and applying to schools.

The broad range of school choice that exists for all students also exists for students with learning difficulties, whether it is a large university in a city or rural setting, or a small liberal arts college in the suburbs. There is also a wide range of student services available regardless of the size or location of the schools. It is important, however, to determine the type of school desired, and then find out which of these has the support that will best suit their needs.

All schools receiving federal funding must be in compliance with IDEA, which means they must provide accommodations for students with documented learning disabilities. Some schools will have whole departments and learning centers for their students. Others will have a mentor or case manager who helps students work with faculty to have their needs met. Some smaller schools will have a culture that is nurturing and supportive of all students that enables those with special needs to thrive. There are also schools that have programs, often at an additional cost, that give direct instruction to students to maximize their adjustment and success to college. These programs act as a bridge between high school and college for students with greater needs. For any of these supportive options to be successful, students must not only be open and available to the interventions, but they should have had the benefit and experience of having advocated for themselves in high school. Students who have become effective advocates accept their disability and recognize and know the accommodations that they need. These are the students that ultimately will be the most successful in school and life.

TIPS and Tools:
Supplementary Materials

Included in this section:

- College Planning
- Self-Advocacy
- Intervention Plan for Smart Kids With Learning Difficulties

College Planning

The checklist that follows should be used by gifted students with learning disabilities when planning for and evaluating college programs.

TIPS

Teacher:
Talk with the school's media specialist or guidance department about purchasing some college reference guides for student and parent use. Organize a program to discuss college choices and available resources. Invite alumni to come and speak with your students and their parents about their experiences of selecting and attending colleges.

Parent:
Be an active participant in the college selection process. Set clear parameters around which your child can make choices, including cost and distance.

Student:
Meet with your guidance counselor in spring of your junior year to begin planning for postsecondary school. Be clear about what you need and want in a school, and begin planning early.

College Planning

Talk to high school counselors or private counselors who work with students with learning difficulties and students who have been through the college search.

Options I am considering:

2-year colleges:

4-year colleges:

Technical:

Level of competitiveness:

Location:

Size:

College Planning, continued

Special services I need in a college:

_____ Departments and learning centers dedicated to serving students
with special needs
_____ Mentors/Case managers
_____ Programs providing direct instruction
_____ Other services I need:_____

_____

_____

_____

Services available at the college I'm considering:

_____ Departments and learning centers dedicated to serving students
with special needs
_____ Mentor/Case managers
_____ Programs providing direct instruction
_____ Other: _____

_____

_____

_____

Notes:

Self-Advocacy

Self-advocacy is when students let others know about who they are and what they need. Learning and practicing strategies for developing self-advocacy make it possible for these students to become risk takers and lifelong learners. Over time, students develop the skills and maturity that allow them to become partners in decision making regarding their Individualized Educational Plans.

TIPS

Teacher:
Use this tool with students to help them identify their strengths and needs. Conference with students so you both gain an understanding of their strengths and needs. Provide an opportunity for students to practice their self-advocacy skills (i.e., role-playing; simulations).

Parent:
Use this tool with your child to help identify strengths and needs. Provide an opportunity for your child to practice self-advocacy skills.

Student:
Fill out the tool sheet. Talk to your parents and teachers and practice self-advocacy skills at home and at school.

Self-Advocacy:
What Defines Me as a Successful Learner?

Who I am (strengths and needs):

_____

_____

_____

_____

_____

_____

What I need (adaptations and accommodations):

_____

_____

_____

_____

_____

Which tools work for me (interventions and strategies)?

_____

_____

_____

_____

_____

_____

How to get what I need to succeed:

_____

_____

_____

_____

_____

_____

Intervention Plan for Smart Kids With Learning Difficulties

The following tool is a sample intervention plan that can be used with gifted and learning-disabled students. Check with your school district, also, as many have preset tools in place for developing intervention plans for students.

TIPS

Teacher:
Use to analyze what is currently in place for the student and to make a plan of what could be done.

Parent:
Use to analyze all aspects of what currently is in place for your child and to make a plan of what could be done.

Student:
Use to understand your strengths and needs and give input to parents and teachers about your plan.

Intervention Plan for Smart Kids
With Learning Difficulties

Name:

Date:

School:

A. Evidence of Gifts:

Test scores:

Performance in school:
(When does the student show interest, perseverance, self-regulation, and outstanding achievement?)

Performance in the community:

Evidence of Learning Difficulties:
(reading, writing, organization, memory, specific learning disabilities, ADHD)

Test scores:

Performance in school:

Behavioral/Attentional Problems:

Performance in school:

Performance at home:

Intervention Plan for Smart Kids With Learning Difficulties, continued

B. Current Program:

Gifted instruction:

Adaptations:

Accommodations:

Special instruction:

Behavior/attention management:
(Plans, medication)

Counseling:
(In-school, therapy)

Case management:
(Home to school communication; communication among staff)

C. Recommendations

Gifted instruction:

Adaptations:

Intervention Plan for Smart Kids With Learning Difficulties, continued

Accommodations:

Special instruction:

Behavior/attention management:

Case management:

D. Next Steps:

CONCLUSION

"Not every child has an equal talent or an equal ability or an equal motivation, but children have the equal right to develop their talent, their ability, and their motivation."

—John F. Kennedy

It is important to think about what the future holds for bright students with learning challenges. A view of the future as seen by Ray Kurzweil (1999) and Thomas West (1997) may shape how these students are educated today. Rapid advances in technology are providing us with a new age of learning and retrieving information. Ray Kurzweil, a brilliant futurist, describes a society in his book, *The Age of Spiritual Machines*, where students interact extensively with computers. He predicts that, by the end of this decade, students will carry thin tablet-like devices for creating and accessing print materials either by voice or by pointing and clicking. Thomas West, in his book, *In the Mind's Eye*, says that it is smart kids with learning difficulties who have made and will make some of the most extraordinary contributions to the world. He predicts that in the 21st century these students, many of whom possess outstanding abstract reasoning and visual-spatial abilities, will take the lead in many important endeavors. Their corresponding weaknesses in rote memory and organization will become insignificant, as technology fulfills those roles.

A majority of the students who have been identified as learning disabled and served during their elementary and secondary years will attend and graduate from college. Many of them will attend universities that are willing and able to provide appropriate accommodations. The majority of these students will experience success in a job that capitalizes on their strengths and interests and many of these students will flourish in careers (including those in the arts, engineering, and the sciences) that capitalize on their strengths and minimize their weaknesses. This knowledge may help shape yours and your child's attitudes regarding the need for appropriate adaptations and accommodations during his elementary and secondary school years.

It is clear that in order to be successful, these students need to have appropriate adaptations and accommodations as they access challenging curriculum and realize their full potential. In order to make the decisions regarding which adaptations and accommodations are appropriate, you, your child, and your child's school need clear guidelines, based on current laws, research, and best practices. Through training, collaborative formulation of educational plans, ongoing communication, and evaluation, you, your child, and his educators will come together to make wise decisions regarding appropriate adaptations, accommodations, programs, and instruction.

As Dr. Ben Carson (2003) said,

> Within every child's brain is a mind teeming with ideas and dreams and abilities unrealized. The greatest thing we can do—as parents, teachers and friends—is to nourish that potential, both intellectual and humani-

tarian, so that each mind can fulfill its promise to the benefit of mankind. (p. 29)

It can be done. Smart students with learning challenges deserve to be, and can be, part of this fulfilled promise.

GLOSSARY

accommodations: procedure or enhancement that empowers a person with a disability to complete a task that he or she would otherwise be unable to complete because of the disability.

adaptations: modification to the delivery of instruction or materials used with a student.

alternative products: giving students choices; examples include oral presentations, models, and other visual representations.

anchor papers: good examples of student work that reflect expectations of the rubric.

arts integration: the inclusion of music, dance, the visual arts, and theatre into English, social studies, science, mathematics, or any subject to enhance the material.

assistive technology: tools that enhance and assist students' ability to achieve individual goals.

audio spell check: computer software that pronounces the word to help with spelling.

audiotape: a recording that enables students to hear print material; a way for students to demonstrate their understanding.

Bloom's Taxonomy: the ordered steps of thinking created by Benjamin Bloom—knowledge, comprehension, application, analysis, synthesis, evaluation.

case management: the process of monitoring a student's instructional program including communication to and among students, parents, and appropriate school staff; monitoring of goals; and scheduling of timely meetings when needed.

CD-ROM: software to help students see and hear information using the computer.

Edward de Bono: one of the leading authors on the process of thinking, who believes thinking is a skill that can be learned, practiced, and improved.

decoding: breaking words down into discreet sounds to facilitate word recognition, pronunciation, and spelling.

differentiation: a kind of instruction that acknowledges commonalities and differences in the teaching and learning process; it is proactive, more qualitative than quantitative, and a blend of whole-class, group, and individual instruction that is student centered.

dramatization: a role-play, skit, reenactment, or simulation.

electronic organizers: a device that helps to organize and plan for upcoming assignments and events.

electronic spellers: a compact device that provides the correct spelling.

empower: behavior that promotes personal growth and increased competencies, increases a person's sense of control over life events, and/or encourages new coping abilities to replace maladaptive behavior (St. Edward's University, n.d.).

enable: behavior that interferes with acquisition of new competencies, reduces a person's sense of self-control over life events (self-efficacy), and/or reinforces old or maladaptive behavior (St. Edward's University, n.d.).

gifted: possessing outstanding abilities in the areas of general intellectual capabilities, specific academic aptitudes, or the arts.

graphic organizer: a visual tool that a student uses to record information, ideas, or concepts to help organize information for prewriting or note taking.

grapho-motor: relating to or affecting movements made in writing.

interdisciplinary approach: a method of teaching that incorporates two or more academic areas that are usually taught separately (i.e., combining history and art or English, science, and social studies).

KWL Chart: a chart used to record what a student knows, wants to learn, and learns about a specific topic.

learning disability: Any of various cognitive, neurological, or psychological disorders that affects the ability to learn, especially one that interferes with the ability to learn mathematics or develop language skills.

metacognition: thinking about thinking, the awareness of one's thinking and cognitive processes.

mind-mapping: a visual tool used to organize one's thinking about a specific topic or concept.

modifications: adjustments made in assignments that address the student's needs/areas of weakness in order to help the student be successful (i.e., shorten assignments, allow a student to dictate rather than write).

mnemonic devices: a tool such as a formula or rhyme used to aid one's memory.

multiple modalities: a combination of senses, such as vision and hearing.

multisensory approach: a style of teaching that incorporates a combination of senses, such as vision, hearing, touch, and kinesthetic.

NCR paper: carbonless copying paper that allows a student to take notes on the top sheet, and transferring it onto a second sheet; useful when a classmate is providing notes for a student with grapho-motor difficulties.

organizational software: computer software that assists students in writing by automatically organizing notes into outline form.

pencil grips: a rubber or sponge-like object that slides on a pencil and provides a better grip for students with grapho-motor difficulties.

portable keyboards: small, relatively inexpensive, lightweight, and durable keyboards that have the capability of storing information, but typically don't have the capacity to install software.

portfolio: an ongoing collection of products, representing a student's best work, and reflecting his or her strengths.

preassessment: a measurement taken before beginning a unit or course of study to determine a student's knowledge and the need for the instruction that is about to occur.

rubric: clearly stated criteria that serves as a means for evaluating students and for guiding their work toward the desired product.

rule-based approach to reading: instruction that is based on students learning and practicing principles that can then be generalized to new material.

scaffolding: a framework to build in necessary subskills that will prepare students for the skill to be taught.

slant board: a tool that eases the physical effort required for handwriting, particularly used for students with grapho-motor issues.

speech-to-text software: computer software that allows the user's speech to be converted directly into print.

spell checker: a computer software program available as part of most writing programs that allows the user to check his or her spelling and replace misspelled words.

storyboards: used professionally by animators and movie makers; the process of students drawing the scenes of a story either as a first step toward writing or as an end product that demonstrates understanding.

story starters: prompts that provide the idea that a student will then elaborate upon in composing a written product.

study guide: a tool for helping students locate and focus upon the information that the teacher has determined is crucial for preparing for an assessment.

task analysis: determination of all of the steps that are required to complete a given work assignment.

text–to–speech software: computer software that allows the user to transfer print material into speech and listen to it.

think alouds: a teaching method that models the problem-solving or thought process that the individual may use to arrive at an answer or solution.

Venn diagram: a specific type of graphic organizer that compares several items and how they relate to one another.

visual imagery: creating pictures in one's mind that serve to clarify concepts and enhance the memory of the concepts.

voice recognition software: another name for speech-to-text software that allows users speech to be converted directly into print.

webs: a specific type of graphic organizer.

word bank: to aide with memory or spelling issues; a list of words provided to the student from which they choose in order to complete a writing assignment or assessment.

word prediction software: computer software that provides alternatives of the words that the user may be looking for after they type the initial letters of a word, or the initial words in a sentence.

REFERENCES

American Psychiatric Association. (2000). *Diagnostic and statistical manual of mental disorders* (4th ed.). Washington, DC: Author.

Barnes-Robinson, L., Jeweler, S., & Ricci, M. C. (2004, June). Potential: Winged possibilities to dreams realized! *Parenting for High Potential*, 20–25.

Barton, J. M., & Starnes, W. T. (1989). Identifying distinguishing characteristics of gifted and talented/learning disabled students. *Roeper Review, 12,* 23–29.

Baum, S. (1984). Meeting the needs of gifted learning disabled students. *Roeper Review, 7,* 16–19.

Baum, S. (1990). *Gifted but learning disabled: A puzzling paradox.* Reston, VA: Council for Exceptional Children. (ERIC Document Reproduction Service No. ED321484)

Baum, S. (2004). *Twice-exceptional and special populations of gifted students.* Thousand Oaks, CA: Corwin Press.

Baum, S., Cooper, C., Neu, T., & Owen, S. V. (1997). *Evaluation of Project High Hopes (Project R206A30159-95)*. Washington, DC: U.S. Department of Education.

Baum, S., Emerick, L., Herman, G., & Dixon, J. (1989). Identification, programs and enrichment strategies for gifted learning disabled youth. *Roeper Review, 12*, 48–53.

Baum, S., Owen, S. V., & Dixon, J. (1991). *To be gifted and learning disabled*. Mansfield Center, CT: Creative Learning Press.

Bloom, B. S., Englehart, M., Furst, E., Hill, W., & Krathwohl, D. (1956). *Taxonomy of educational objectives: The classification of educational goals. Handbook 1: Cognitive Domain*. New York: Longmans, Green.

Borenson, H. (1997). *Hands-on equations*. Allentown, PA: Borenson and Associates.

Brody, L. E., & Mills, C. J. (1997). Gifted children with learning disabilities: A review of the issues. *Journal of Learning Disabilities, 30*, 282–297.

Burton, J., Horowitz, R., & Abeles, H. (1999). Learning in and through the arts: Curriculum implications. In T. Fisk (Ed.), *Champions of change*. Washington, DC: Arts Education Partnership.

Carson, B. (2003, December 7). Your mind can map your destiny. *Parade Magazine*, 28–30.

Cline, S., & Schwartz, D. (1999). *Diverse populations of gifted children*. Englewood Cliffs, NJ: Merrill/Prentice Hall.

College of William and Mary Center for Gifted Education. (1998) *Literary reflections: Language arts units for high-ability learners. Novel assignment, Handout 3B*. Dubuque, IA: Kendall/Hunt Publishing.

Council for Exceptional Children. (2000). *Making assessment accommodations: A toolkit for educators*. Reston, VA: Author.

deBono, E. (1986). *Six thinking hats*. New York: Little Brown and Company.

Dix, J., & Schafer, S. (1996). From paradox to performance. *Gifted Child Today, 19*, 22–29.

Fisk, T. B. (Ed.). (1999). *Champions of change*. Washington, DC: Arts Education Partnership.

Friend, M. (1996) *The power of two: Making a difference through co-teaching*. Port Chester, NY: National Educational Resources.

Fuchs, L. S., Fuchs, D., Eaton, S. B., Hamlett, C., & Karns, K. (2000). Supplementing teacher judgments of mathematics test accommodations with objective data sources. *School Psychology Review, 29*, 65–85.

Gardner, H. (1983). *Frames of mind: The theory of multiple intelligences.* New York: Basic Books.

Higgins, D., Baldwin, L., & Pereles, D. (2000). *Comparison of characteristics of gifted students with or without disabilities.* Unpublished manuscript.

Individuals with Disabilities Education Act, 20 U.S.C. §1401 et seq. (1990).

Jeweler, S., & Barnes-Robinson, L., (1999). Curriculum from a conflict-resolution perspective. *Kappa Delta Pi Record, 35*(3), 112–116.

Kurzweil, R. (1999). *The age of spiritual machines: When computers exceed human intelligence.* New York: Penguin.

Landrum, T. J. (1989). Gifted and learning disabled students: Practical considerations for teachers. *Academic Therapy, 24,* 533–545.

Lenz, K., & Schumaker, J. (1999). *Adapting language arts, social studies, and science materials for the inclusive classroom: Volume 3: Grades six through eight.* Reston, VA: Council for Exceptional Children.

Maryland State Department of Education. (1999). *Maryland state performance assessment program.* Baltimore, MD: Author.

Maryland State Department of Education. (2000). *Requirements for accommodating, excusing, and exempting students in Maryland assessment programs.* Baltimore, MD: Author.

Maryland State Department of Education. (2001). *Identifying specific learning disabilities.* Baltimore, MD: Author.

Maryland Task Force on Gifted and Talented Education. (1994). *Renewing our commitment to the education of gifted and talented students: An essential component of educational reform.* Baltimore, MD: Maryland State Department of Education.

McAlpine, J., Weincek, B., Jeweler, S., & Finkbinder, M. (1982). *CPS: Planning new worlds.* New York: Sunburst Communications.

Montgomery County Public Schools. (1994). *Conflict resolution tools: Elementary version, teaching through the curriculum.* Rockville, MD: Author.

Mooney, J., & Cole, D. (2000). *Learning outside the lines: Two Ivy League students with learning disabilities and ADHD give you the tools for academic success and educational revolution.* New York: Fireside.

National Association for Gifted Children. (1998). *Students with concomitant gifts and learning disabilities* (NAGC Position Paper). Washington, DC: Author.

No Child Left Behind Act, 20 U.S.C. §6301 (2001).

Olsen, J. Z. (2002). *Handwriting without tears.* Cabin John, MD: Author.

Reis, S. M., & McCoach, D. B. (2000). The underachievement of gifted students: What do we know and where do we go? *Gifted Child Quarterly, 44,* 152–170.

Renzulli, J. S. (1977). *The enrichment triad model: A guide for developing defensible programs for the gifted and talented.* Mansfield Center, CT: Creative Learning Press.

Renzulli, J. S., & Reis, S. M. (1997). *The schoolwide enrichment model: A how-to guide for educational excellence.* Mansfield Center, CT: Creative Learning Press.

Section 504 of the Rehabilitation Act, 29 U.S.C. Section 706 et. seq. (1973).

Shevitz, B., Weinfeld, R., Jeweler, S., & Barnes-Robinson, L. (2003) Mentoring empowers gifted/learning disabled students to soar. *Roeper Review, 26,* 37–40.

Silverman, L. K. (1989). Invisible gifts, invisible handicaps. *Roeper Review, 12,* 37–41.

St. Edward's University. (n.d.). *Enabling versus empowering.* Retrieved December 2, 2005, from http://www.stedwards.edu/cte/resources/enabling.htm

Starnes, W., Ginevan, J., Stokes, L., & Barton, J. (1988, March). *A study in the identification, differential diagnosis, and remediation of under-achieving highly able students.* Paper presented at annual meeting of the Council for Exceptional Children, Washington, DC.

Thurlow, M., House, A., Scott, D., & Ysseldyke, J. (2001). *State participation and accommodation policies for students with disabilities.* Minneapolis, MN: National Center for Educational Outcomes.

Tindal, G., & Fuchs, L. (1999). *A summary of research on test changes: An empirical basis for defining accommodations.* Lexington, KY: MidSouth Regional Resource Center.

Title IV, Part B. [Jacob K. Javits Gifted and Talented Students Education Act of 1988], Elementary and Secondary Education Act of 1988, 20 U.S.C. ° 3061 et seq.

Tomlinson, C. A. (1999). *The differentiated classroom: Responding to the needs of all learners.* Alexandria, VA: ASCD.

Tomlinson, C. A. (2000). *Differentiation of instruction in the elementary grades.* Reston, VA: ERIC Clearinghouse on Disabilities and Gifted Education. (ERIC Document Reproduction Service No. ED443572)

VanTassel-Baska, J. (1991). Serving the disabled gifted through educational collaboration. *Journal for the Education of the Gifted, 14,* 246–266.

Weinfeld, R., Barnes-Robinson, L., Jeweler, S., & Shevitz, B. (2002). Academic programs for gifted and talented/learning disabled students. *Roeper Review, 24,* 226–233.

West, T. G. (1991) *In the mind's eye: Visual thinkers, gifted people with learning difficulties, computer images, and the ironies of creativity.* Buffalo, NY: Prometheus Books.

West Chester Area School District v. Chad C., 194 F.sup.2d 417 (E.D.Pa.2002).

Whitmore, J. R. (1980). *Giftedness, conflict, and underachievement.* Boston: Allyn & Bacon.

Whitmore, J. R. (1981). Gifted children with handicapping conditions: A new frontier. *Exceptional Children, 48,* 106–113.

Willard-Holt, C. (1999, May). *Dual exceptionalities.* ERIC EC Digest #574. Reston, VA: ERIC Clearinghouse on Disabilities and Gifted Education.

RESOURCES

Print Resources:

Alley, G., & Deschler, D. (1979). *Teaching the learning disabled adolescent: Strategies and methods.* Denver: Love Publishing.

Baldwin, L. J., & Gargiulo, D. A. (1983). A model program for elementary age learning disabled/gifted youngsters. In L. H. Fox, L. Brody, & D. Tobin (Eds.), *Learning disabled/gifted children: Identification and programming* (pp. 207–221). Austin, TX: PROED.

Baum, S. (1994). Meeting the needs of gifted/learning disabled students: How far have we come? *Journal of Secondary Gifted Education, 5,* 6–16.

Beckley, D. (1998). *Gifted and learning disabled: Twice exceptional students.* Storrs, CT: The National Research Center on the Gifted and Talented.

Bees, C. (1998). The GOLD program: A program for gifted learning disabled adolescents. *Roeper Review, 21*, 155–161

Betts, G. T. (1985). *Autonomous learner model.* Greeley, CO: ALPS.

Clements, C., Lundell, F., & Hishinuma, E. S. (1994). Serving the gifted dyslexic and gifted at risk. *Gifted Child Today, 17(4)*, 12–14, 16–17, 36–37.

Coleman, M. R., & Gallagher, J. J. (1995). State identification policies: Gifted students from special populations. *Roeper Review, 17*, 268–275.

Daniels, P. R. (1983). *Teaching the gifted/learning disabled child.* Rockville, MD: Aspen Press.

deBono, E. (1986). *The CoRT thinking program.* Easterville, OH: SRA.

Dunst, C., & Trivette, C. (1987). Enabling and empowering families: Conceptual and intervention issues. *School Psychology Review, 16*, 443–456.

Ellston, T. (1993). Gifted and learning disabled . . . a paradox? *Gifted Child Today, 16*, 17–19.

Fall, J., & Nolan, L. (1993). A paradox of personalities. *Gifted Child Today, 16*, 46–49.

Fetzer, E. (2000). The gifted/learning-disabled child: A guide for teachers and parents. *Gifted Child Today, 23(4)*, 44–50.

Fine, L. (2001a). Diamonds in the rough. *Education Week, XXI(8)*, 38, 39, 41.

Fine, L. (2001b). Mining Maryland's diamonds: One district's solution. *Education Week, XXI(8)*, 40.

Fox, L. H., Brody, L., & Tobin, D. (Eds.). (1983). *Learning disabled/gifted children: Identification and programming.* Austin, TX: PROED.

Gentry, M., & Neu, T. W. (1998). Project High Hopes summer institute: Curriculum for developing talent in students with special needs. *Roeper Review, 20*, 291–295.

Grimm, J. (1998). The participation of gifted students with disabilities in gifted programs. *Roeper Review, 20*, 285–286.

Hammill, D. D. (1990). On defining learning disabilities: An emerging consensus. *Journal of Learning Disabilities, 23*, 74–84.

Hishinuma, E. S., & Nishimura, S. T. (2000). Parent attitudes on the importance and success of integrated self-contained services for students who are gifted, learning disabled, and gifted/learning disabled. *Roeper Review, 22*, 241–250.

Howard, J. B. (1994). Addressing needs through strengths: Five instructional practices for use with gifted/learning disabled students. *Journal of Secondary Gifted Education. 5*, 23–34.

LeVine, E., & Evans, M. J. (1983). The behaviorally disordered creative child: A challenge to our diagnostic and teaching procedures. *Contemporary Education, 55,* 28–32.

Maker, C. J. (1977). *Providing programs for the gifted handicapped.* Reston, VA: Council for Exceptional Children.

Maker, C. J. (1981). Problem solving strategies: A general approach to remediation. In D. D. Smith (Ed.), *Teaching the learning disabled* (pp. 132–166). Englewood Cliffs, NJ: Prentice-Hall.

Marland, S. P. (1972). *Education of the gifted and talented* (Report to the subcommittee on education, Committee on Labor and Public Welfare, U.S. Senate). Washington, DC: U.S. Government Printing Office.

Montgomery County Public Schools. (1998). *State of the art.* Rockville, MD: Author.

Montgomery County Public Schools (1994). *Conflict resolution tools: Elementary version, teaching through the curriculum.* Rockville, MD: Author.

Montgomery County Public Schools. (2004). *Twice-exceptional students: A guidebook for supporting the achievement of gifted students with special needs.* Rockville, MD: Author.

Nielsen, M. E., Higgins, L. D., Wilkinson, S. C., & Webb, K. W. (1994). Helping twice-exceptional students to succeed in high school. *Journal of Secondary Gifted Education, 5,* 35–39.

Nielsen, M. E., & Mortorff-Albert, S. (1989). The effects of special education service on the self-concept and school attitude of learning disabled/gifted students. *Roeper Review, 12,* 29–35.

Norton, S., Hartwell-Hunnicut, K., & Norton, R. (1996). The learning disabled/gifted student. *Contemporary Education, 68,* 36–40.

Ogle, D. M. (1986). K-W-L: A teaching model that develops action reading of expository text. *The Reading Teacher, 40,* 564–570.

Putnum/Northern Westchester Board of Cooperative Educational Services. (n.d.). *The gifted handicapped mentor program.* Yorktown Heights, NY: Author.

Reis, S. M., Neu, T. W. & McGuire, J. M. (1995). *Talents in two places: Case studies of high ability students with learning disabilities who have achieved* (Research Monograph 95114). Storrs, CT: The National Research Center on the Gifted and Talented.

Rivera, D. B., Murdock, J., & Sexton, D. (1995). Serving the gifted/ learning disabled. *Gifted Child Today, 18(6),* 34–37.

Southern, W. T., & Jones, E. D. (1991). *The academic acceleration of gifted children.* New York: Teachers College Press.

Suter, D. P., & Wolf, J. S. (1987). Issues in the identification and programming of the gifted/learning disabled child. *Journal for the Education of the Gifted, 10,* 227–237.

Thrailkrill, C. (1998). Patrick's story: A gifted/learning-disabled child. *Gifted Child Today, 21(3)*, 24–27.

Torgesen, J. K. (1986). Computer assisted instruction with learning disabled students. In J. K. Torgesen & B. Y. L. Wong (Eds.), *Psychological and educational perspectives on learning disabilities* (pp. 417–435). Orlando, FL: Academic Press.

Udall, A. J., & Maker, C. J. (1983). A pilot program for elementary age learning disabled/gifted students. In L. H. Fox, L. Brody, & D. Tobin (Eds.), *Learning disabled/gifted children: Identification and programming* (pp. 223–242). Austin, TX: PROED.

Vaughn, S. (1989). Gifted learning disabilities: Is it such a bright idea? *Learning Disabilities Focus, 4*, 123–126.

Waldron, K. A., Saphire, D. G., & Rosenblum, S. A. (1987). Learning disabilities and giftedness: Identification based on self-concept. *Journal of Learning Disabilities, 20*, 422–432.

Whitmore, J., & Maker, J. (1985). *Intellectual giftedness in disabled persons.* Rockville, MD: Aspen Press.

Will, M. (1986). *Educating students with learning problems: A shared responsibility.* Washington, DC: U.S. Department of Education.

Webb, J. T., & Latimer, D. (1993). *ADHD and children who are gifted.* ERIC EC Digest #E522. Reston, VA: ERIC Clearinghouse on Disabilities and Gifted Education.

Winebrenner, S. (1996). *Teaching kids with learning difficulties in the regular classroom.* Minneapolis, MN: Free Spirit.

Yewchuk, C., & Bibby, M. A. (1988). A comparison of parent and teacher nomination of gifted hearing-impaired students. *American Annals of the Deaf, 133*, 344–348.

Web Sites:

2e (Twice-Exceptional) Newsletter
http://www.2enewsletter.com

All Kinds of Minds
http://www.allkindsofminds.org

Association for the Education of Gifted Underachieving Students
http://www.aegus.org

Autism Society of America
http://www.autism-society.org

Center For Talented Youth, Johns Hopkins University
http://www.jhu.edu/~gifted

Children and Adults With Attention Deficit/Hyperactivity Disorder
http://www.chadd.org

Council for Exceptional Children
http://www.cec.sped.org

Dyscalculia (math learning disability)
http://www.dyscalculia.org

Educational Research & Information Center (ERIC)
http://www.ericec.org

Gifted Development Center
http://www.gifteddevelopment.com

GT World
http://www.gtworld.org

Hoagies' Gifted Education
http://www.hoagiesgifted.org

International Dyslexia Society
http://interdys.org

LD Online
http://www.ldonline.org

Learning Disabilities Association of America
http://www.ldanatl.org

National Association for Gifted Children
http://www.nagc.org

National Center for Learning Disabilities
http://www.ncld.org

National Dissemination Center for Children With Disabilities
http://www.nichcy.org

NLD on the Web!
http://www.nldontheweb.org

Nonverbal Learning Disorders Association
http://www.nlda.org

Parent Encouragement Program
http://www.parentencouragement.org

Schwab Learning
http://www.SchwabLearning.org

Smart Kids With Learning Disabilities
http://www.smartkidswithld.org

The Gifted With Learning Differences Educational Network
http://www.gtldnetwork.org

Uniquely Gifted
http://www.uniquelygifted.org

Wrightslaw Libraries
http://www.wrightslaw.com

ABOUT THE AUTHORS

Rich Weinfeld has long been an advocate for appropriate educational programming for all students. He currently provides advocacy to parents of students with a wide range of learning challenges, training to parents and staff on various educational topics, and consultation to schools and school systems regarding appropriate programming for all students. Rich serves on the national board of directors of the Association for Educators of Gifted Underachieving Students (AEGUS).

He previously served as Montgomery County (Maryland) Public School's first full-time Instructional Specialist for Gifted and Talented/Learning Disabled Programs. Rich has presented many workshops regarding best educational practices that help all students to succeed. He has also coauthored several articles regarding programming for smart kids with learning challenges.

Rich received his bachelor's degree from American University and his master's degree from Trinity College. He is certified in administration and supervision. For more information about his current endeavors, visit his Web site at http://www.richweinfeld.com.

Sue Jeweler spent her 30-year career in Maryland's Montgomery County Public Schools (MCPS) teaching elementary school; training student teachers from area universities; training teachers in conflict-resolution strategies, gifted and talented instruction, differentiation, and accommodation strategies; and in writing conflict resolution and social studies curricula.

Sue has been a consultant to the Kennedy Center, the Smithsonian Institute, National Geographic, Berns & Kay, and Street Law. She has coauthored two educational kits, more than 30 books, and numerous articles for journals and magazines. She has received many awards, including the prestigious *Washington Post* Agnes Meyer Outstanding Teaching Award. She received her bachelor's degree from the University of Maryland. Sue is married with children and one grandchild.

Linda Barnes-Robinson has worked with children and parents for more than 25 years, and has devoted her professional life to advocating for children and families. With Montgomery County Public Schools, she coordinated the identification of gifted and talented students, advocated for parents and students, and worked to establish one of the first comprehensive programs for gifted/learning-disabled students in the nation.

Linda is a nationally recognized trainer and educational consultant in gifted identification, gifted/learning-disabled programs, and conflict resolution and mediation. She has coauthored and edited numerous articles, manuals, books, and curricula documents. Her most recent publications include two articles for the journal *Teaching Exceptional Children*.

She received her bachelor's degree from Cedar Crest College, her master's degree from The George Washington University, and a postgraduate certificate in family mediation from The Catholic University of America.

Betty Roffman Shevitz has 25 years of experience with gifted students. She currently serves as an instructional specialist for gifted students in Montgomery County Public Schools and is responsible for the screening and identification of students for seven centers for the highly gifted. In addition, Ms. Shevitz coordinates the Wings Mentor Program, a countywide program she codeveloped to support students who are both gifted and learning disabled.

Betty has directed her attention to special populations, and is dedicated to helping nurture students' potential. She has worked with school systems in Virginia, Minnesota, Texas, and Maryland. She has extensive experience both in the classroom and in the central office of school districts with large populations of gifted students. She was involved in the initial year of a program designed for identifying and nurturing gifted students in underserved populations. In addition to classroom experience, Betty has developed curricula, presented at national and state conferences, and served as an educational consultant and a teacher trainer. She also served as a member of the Olympic Educational Program Curriculum Committee for Visions of Glory, an education program for the 1988 Winter Games.

Betty received her bachelor's degree in education and her master's degree in gifted education from the University of Virginia.

For more information, or to contact the authors, visit http://www.smartkidsresource.com.